QUICK STUDIES
Philippians–Hebrews

DAVID C. COOK PUBLISHING CO.
ELGIN, ILLINOIS—WESTON, ONTARIO

The following authors and editors contributed to this volume:

Stan Campbell
Jane Vogel
John Duckworth
Jim Townsend, Ph.D.

Quick Studies
Philippians through Hebrews

© 1992 David C. Cook Publishing Co.

Published by David C. Cook Publishing Co.
850 North Grove Ave., Elgin, IL 60120
Cable address: DCCOOK
Designed by Bill Paetzold
Cover illustrations by Steve Bjorkman
Inside illustrations by Paul Turnbaugh, Jack DesRocher, and John Duckworth
Printed in U.S.A.

ISBN: 0-7814-0028-7

CONTENTS

Quick Questions about Quick Studies

We've made *Quick Studies* as self-explanatory as possible, so you can dive in and start using them right away. But just in case you were wondering . . .

When should I use *Quick Studies*?

Whenever you want high school or junior high kids to explore the Bible face-to-face and absorb it into their lives. We've kept the openers active and the discussion questions creative, so you can use *Quick Studies* with confidence in Sunday school, midweek youth Bible study, small groups, even youth group meetings and retreats.

What's so quick about *Quick Studies*?

They're designed to save you preparation time. The session plans are compact, for quick reading. There aren't a lot of materials to gather, either (you'll need Bibles, pencils and paper, copies of the reproducible sheets, and sometimes a few other items). Yet *Quick Studies* are *real* Bible studies, with plenty of thought-provoking discussion and life application.

How are these different from other youth Bible studies?

We like to think *Quick Studies* are . . .

• *Irresistible.* You already know most kids don't jump at the chance to fill in a bunch of blanks in a boring study guide. So we used creative, reproducible sheets and *active* activities to draw kids into Scripture.

• *Involving.* You need discussion *starters*, not discussion *stoppers*. We avoided dull "yes or no" questions and included lots of thought-provokers that should get your group members talking about important issues. And we didn't forget suggested *answers* to most of the tougher questions, which should make things easier for you.

• *Inductive.* Many Bible studies try to force-feed kids a single "aim" and ignore other points Scripture is trying to make. *Quick Studies* let kids discover a variety of key principles in a passage.

• *Influential.* It's not enough to know what the Bible says. Every session includes a step designed to help kids decide what to do *personally* with vital points from the chapter.

When do kids read the passages covered?

That's up to you. If your group is into homework, assign the passages in advance. If not, take time to read the Scripture together after the "Opening Act" step that kicks off each session. There are dozens of ways to read a passage—with volunteers taking turns, or with a narrator and actors "performing" a scene, or with kids underlining points as they read silently, or with you reading as the author and kids listening as the original audience, or with small groups paraphrasing as they read . . .

What if I want to cover more—or less—than a chapter in a session?

Quick Studies is flexible. Each 45-to 60-minute session covers a chapter of the New Testament, but you can adjust the speed to fit your group. To cover more than one chapter in a session, just pick the points you want to emphasize and drop the activities, questions, and reproducible sheets you don't need. To cover less than a chapter, you may need to add a few questions and spend more time discussing the "So What?" application step in detail.

Do I have to cover a whole New Testament book?

No. Each session stands alone. Use sessions one at a time if you want to, or mix and match books in any order you choose. No matter how you use them, *Quick Studies* are likely to help your group see Bible study in a whole new light.

John Duckworth, Series Editor

You've Only Just Begun

CHAPTER ✓ CHECK

The apostle Paul, while under house arrest, writes the Philippian church to thank its people for their support. He gives them an update on his own circumstances, and challenges them to remain faithful to Jesus and His Gospel—no matter what happens.

OPENING ACT

(Needed: Paper and markers, prizes [all optional])

Introduce the idea of "carrying on to completion" (vs. 6) with one or more of the following. *Option 1:* Form teams and pick two strong members of each team to serve as carriers. Have them form a "chair" by crossing their hands and racing to carry all their team members across a finish line. (If you have a small group, race against the clock.) *Option 2:* Form teams to create assembly-line portraits of famous people. Give each person a marker and each team several sheets of paper. When you call out the name of a celebrity, each team member contributes one or more features (a nose, or hair and chin) before passing the sheet to the next person. Award prizes for fastest drawing and best portraits if you like.

Michael Jordan
President Clinton
Steve Eurkiel
Bugs
Shag
Reggie

DATE I USED THIS SESSION _1-29-95_ GROUP I USED IT WITH _Michael, Shelley, Gina_

NOTES FOR NEXT TIME _____

_____

_____

Q&A

1. When you think of your close friends and family members, do you ever stop to thank God for them (vss. 1-3)? Or do you usually take them for granted? What are some things about those people that you *could* thank God for?

2. Do you ever think of Christian friends as "partners in the gospel" (vs. 5)? Why or why not? What's one thing you've accomplished with the help of another Christian?

3. How can you tell whether God has begun a "good work" in you (vs. 6)? (He has if you've received Christ as Savior; if the Holy Spirit lives in you and influences your life; if your attitudes and actions are growing more Christlike than they were when you received Christ.) **How can you tell that it isn't yet complete?**

4. Paul was a prisoner when he wrote this letter. If you were being held in prison for an indefinite time, would you write any letters? To whom? Would your letters be angry, creative, funny, or serious? What would you want your friends and family members to know in case you never came home? How does this compare with Paul's letter to the Philippians?

5. You've probably never been imprisoned for talking about Jesus (vss. 7, 8). **What's the most you've suffered because of your faith? Did the experience make you more confident or less confident?** (Suffering for what we believe often increases faith. If we struggle to avoid suffering [as Jonah did], our faith won't grow.)

6. Paul used words like "best," "pure," and "blameless" (vss. 9-11) to describe the way we should be. Do these sound too extreme to you? Why do you think he didn't use words like "adequate," "fair," and "just good enough"? (Paul is talking about a process of becoming more like Jesus, and says that God is in charge of that process [vs. 6]. Maybe we set lower goals because we try to reach them on our own.]

7. When Paul was imprisoned for spreading the Gospel, it only drew more attention to him. Others "on the outside" spoke up in his place, while his guards became

Paul's new audience (vss. 12-14). **Can you think of a time when you or someone else was in a bad situation but something good came of it?** (Examples: A dying friend whose constant faith was clear to others; a house burns down and a youth group rallies to help the family.)

8. What did Paul think about the preachers of his day who were spreading Christianity for the wrong reasons (vss. 15-18)? How do you feel about Christians who are getting things done, but whose style—clothes, way of worshiping, etc.—is very different from yours? (Aside from illegal or immoral practices, we need not be overly concerned about such people as long as the Gospel is spread.)

9. Paul knew the future held two options for him: to keep on telling about Jesus or to die. He could hardly decide which he'd prefer—not because both were so scary, but because he thought both were so good (vss. 19-26)! How would you feel if those were your only options?

10. Paul said, "For me to live is . . ." (vs. 21). How did he finish that phrase? How would most people you know finish it? How would you? Do the same with the phrase, "to die is . . ."

11. Based on verses 27-30, how would you answer the charge that Christianity is for weaklings? (Christians need to be tough to face opposition and suffering. We have access to God's strength to help us act in a worthy way, stand firm, and not be frightened [vss. 27-30].)

The reproducible sheet, "I'm Not Done Yet!" will give kids a starting point for measuring their growth in several areas of Christian living. Discuss responses as kids are willing. Ask: **How has God been "baking" you so far? Have you ever felt "overcooked"? Why? How could the rest of us help you stay "in the oven"?** If possible, try to agree on one area to work on as a group during the next month or so. Focus on continuing growth, knowing that God ensures the completion.

I'm Not Done Yet!

When it comes to really following Jesus, do you ever feel half-baked? Well, you're still cooking! Sometimes God lets the heat get turned up pretty high to make sure you're getting "done." But He promises not to leave you unfinished—at least as long as you're willing to stay in the "oven."

In each of the categories below, how "baked" are you? Check your "doneness" on the chart.

RAW	BARELY WARM	HALF-BAKED	ALMOST DONE	DONE	BURNED

Thanking God for other Christians

Praying joyfully

Feeling like a partner with other believers

Being confident that God's still working on me

Caring more about God's plans than my plans

Talking about Jesus without fear

Being glad that other Christians are spreading the good news about Jesus, even if they go about it in ways I don't agree with

Letting Christ be the most important person or thing in my life

Not being afraid to die

Encouraging other Christians

Conducting myself in a way that fits a follower of Jesus

Standing firm against anyone who doesn't want me to obey God

Being ready and willing to suffer for following Jesus

"Being confident of this, that He who began a good work in you will carry it on to completion until the day of Christ Jesus" (Philippians 1:6).

PHILIPPIANS 2

Downwardly Mobile

Paul explains to the Philippians that the key to unity is humility. As we follow Jesus' example and become more concerned with others' needs than with our own, God is honored and He takes care of us. Two good examples are Timothy and Epaphroditus.

Ask group members to perform some of their favorite sports cheers. Look specifically for examples of the "Fight! Kill! Win!" mentality. Then divide into teams and ask kids to write and perform some cheers for "Humble High," a new school in town where the emphasis is more on serving and doing your best than on winning. Challenge them to be as creative as possible and to have fun. Then discuss the results, which may reveal kids' attitudes toward humility and competition.

DATE I USED THIS SESSION _2-5-95_ GROUP I USED IT WITH _Michael_

NOTES FOR NEXT TIME _needs a group_

1. Think of the last major fight or argument you had. What caused it?

2. Do you ever sense God's encouragement, comfort, fellowship, tenderness, or compassion (vs. 1)? How? If you have, what should you do? (Vss. 2-4—These characteristics, given in abundance by God, should prompt us to get along with each other.)

3. What percentage of people at your school would you say try to put the interests of others above their own and consider others better than themselves? Are you included in that percentage?

4. If God has made everyone to be of equal value, why would He want us to think of others as better than ourselves? Won't that hurt us? (Paul doesn't say that anyone is really better than anyone else. He wants us to put others' needs ahead of our own.)

5. How could such unselfish behavior on your part bring joy to anyone else (vs. 2)? (We might be surprised at how impressed teachers, youth leaders, and even fellow students would be with anyone who really was humble.)

6. Read verses 5-11 and notice the results of Christ's humility. What do you think the results will be if you are truly humble? (Jesus temporarily lost the comfort and privileges of heaven; He was given a hard time by a lot of hard-hearted people; He died an excruciating and humiliating death; He gave Himself for the entire world's sins; and He was exalted by God to the highest place possible. Humility is not always pleasant, yet God will reward it.)

7. During the last week or so, when did you face a choice to be humble—and chose not to be? What happened? What might have happened if you'd chosen differently?

8. If you were writing music to go with verses 6-11, what moods would it go through? At what points would you change moods? Why?

9. What does it mean to "work out your salvation with fear and trembling" (vs. 12)? (This seems to mean expressing your salvation through action more and more—not that you're saved by your work. "Fear and trembling" may be our reaction to realizing how dependent we are on God [vs. 13].)

10. We have a chance to be stars (vs. 15)! How might following the instructions in verses 14-18 make us stand out? (As we refuse to argue or complain—and as we let others know who is influencing our behavior—we'll be noticed by those around us.)

11. We all know Paul was a special case. Can we really expect to live up to his (and God's) standards? (Vss. 19-24—Yes, we can with God's help. If students don't seem convinced, point out that Timothy was a young person who exhibited the same godly characteristics.)

12. Some people get cranky and selfish when they're sick. But Epaphroditus [vss. 25-30] was concerned during his near-death illness that his friends might find out and be upset. When is it toughest for you to be humble—when you're sick, when you've gotten an award, when things don't go your way, or when things go badly for an enemy of yours?

Teenagers have a hard time dealing with humility. They struggle with insecurity and are desperate to develop self-confidence. Make it clear that an attitude of *humility* does not have to mean perpetual *humiliation*. The case studies on the reproducible sheet, "Humility vs. Stupidity," should generate discussion in this direction. Proper responses may not be obvious, so let group members explain why they would act as they say they would. Follow the discussion with positive reinforcement for the things your kids are doing right.

Humility vs Stupidity

"Your attitude should be the same as that of Christ Jesus" (Philippians 2:5).

Most of us could use more humility. Yet Jesus, in all His humility, never stopped using His head. He got angry on occasion—with just cause. He made bold, sometimes harsh statements when faced with people who would mislead children, use religion for their own purposes, or oppose God's will. So showing humility doesn't always mean letting anyone and everyone stomp over you with football cleats.

What do you think would be the right, *humble* thing to do in each of the following situations?

1. Three obnoxious kids cut in front of you in the cafeteria line without saying a word.

_____

_____

2. You're serving on a student council committee with some older kids. A couple of them take God's name in vain during every other sentence or so, and they don't seem to realize they're offending anyone.

_____

_____

3. You get a *C-* on a major English assignment that you really thought was an *A* paper. You had worked very hard on it.

_____

_____

4. You witness a drug transaction right after school. The kids involved realize that you've seen them, but one mutters, "Hey, no problem." He then turns to you and says, "This is our business, not yours. So stay out of it!"

_____

_____

5. You accidentally stumble into the school bully, who spills part of a can of pop on himself or herself. He or she responds by shoving you into the lockers.

_____

_____

Go for the Gold

Paul warns about people who get too legalistic, using his own background as proof that Christianity involves much more than outward appearance and training. Then he challenges his readers to keep pressing toward the goal—heaven, where we have our citizenship.

(Needed: Scrap paper and two wastebaskets or large boxes)

Form two teams and give each team a stack of scrap paper. Designate a boundary between the two teams. Place a goal (an empty wastebasket or box) in each team's territory; give kids about thirty seconds to wad up their paper and shoot as many pieces as possible into the goal in the other team's territory. It's OK to try to block the other team's shots, but designate a "no trespass" area around each goal so it can't be completely blocked. After the game (and cleanup), explain that this chapter will talk about trying for a goal in spite of interference.

DATE I USED THIS SESSION 2-12-95   GROUP I USED IT WITH Adam, Gina, & Michael

NOTES FOR NEXT TIME

Help
Bored
Escape Route

1. If you were imprisoned and separated from your friends, what four words might go through your mind most often? (Possibilities: Escape, hopeless, trapped, help, hate, etc. See whether anyone would include "Rejoice in the Lord" [vs. 1] among the comments.)

2. Paul seems more concerned about his friends than about himself. He warns them about a group who thought circumcision should be required of every male believer, Jewish or Gentile (vss. 2-4). What are some things that certain Christians think all believers should have to do today? (Stick to dress codes; use certain translations of the Bible; worship in a certain way, etc.) What are some things that certain Christians think all believers must avoid? (Alcohol, movies, dancing, etc.)

3. Was Paul saying that Christians shouldn't have to follow any rules? (No. He was against putting "confidence in the flesh" [vs. 4], or believing that rule-following can save you. Only faith in Christ can save anyone.)

4. What gave Paul the right to criticize these other people? (Vss. 4-6—He was not only born and raised as a good Jew, but was also educated and hard-working. He knew what he was talking about.) You probably don't have the background that Paul had, but what are some good things about you that you might be tempted to think make you fit for heaven? (Being a Christian for a long time; going to church faithfully; helping someone else become a Christian; knowing a lot about the Bible; being a model student, etc.)

5. Paul thought the things he'd lost were worthless garbage compared to knowing Christ (vss. 7, 8). Do you think he (a) was exaggerating, (b) said that because he couldn't have those things back anyway, (c) had been a prisoner for too long, or (d) had another reason? Explain.

6. If Paul ever wrote New Year's resolutions, he probably put verses 10 and 11 at the top of his list. In your own words, what did Paul want to know and become? (He wanted to know Christ better and see God's power—which was strong enough to raise Jesus from the dead—working in his own life. He wanted to stand up for Christ even though he might have to suffer and die as Jesus did. Paul also wanted to overcome death and live forever, as Jesus promised to His followers.)

7. **What are some of your long-range goals? How do you regularly measure your progress toward your goals?** (Examples: Grades on report cards; weight scales; number of roles in school plays; home runs in baseball, etc.) **How do your goals compare with Paul's?**

8. **Paul described the process of Christian growth as "press[ing] on toward the goal to win the prize"** (vss. 12, 14). **If and when you became a Christian, was there any talk of all this pressing and straining? Do you think following Jesus is more like pushing a two-ton boulder up a hill by yourself, rowing a boat as part of a team, or being driven in a limousine? Why?**

9. **What percentage of kids in all the church youth groups would you say really want to mature as Christians? What percentage are better described by verses 18 and 19?**

10. **What difference does it make if your citizenship is in heaven** (vs. 20)? (You should make choices on the basis of what the results might be years [and even thousands of years] from now, when you're with God. If you think of earth as a "temporary residence," you may not be as likely to make bad decisions based on shortsighted thinking.) **If you begin to think of yourself as a citizen of heaven, what changes might you need to make in your plans for next week? Next year?**

The reproducible sheet, "Pressing on for the Prize," asks kids to evaluate their proficiency in several spiritual "events." After they award themselves appropriate medals in each of the events, discuss: **Which of these things comes most naturally for you? Which is hardest? Why? Do you think God expects you to excel in each of these? Do you think He at least expects you to compete?**

Pressing on for the Prize

At a track meet it's easy to tell how well you do. You compete against a certain number of people, and the two or three winners get trophies, medals, or ribbons. But if Christianity is like running a race, the rules are different. You cross the "finish line" when you die. You may win a "prize" from God, but you're running to finish—not to compete against others.

So to help you measure your progress so far, here are some spiritual "athletic events." For each one, circle a first, second, or third place ribbon—or an "X" for "nothing at all"—to show what you think you'd deserve if you crossed the finish line today.

The Marathon—Have you developed enough stamina to set a pace and make progress over a long period in becoming more like Jesus? The pace need not be quick, but it should be consistent.

The Hurdles—Do you overcome obstacles with God's help—and learn from the experience? You may not leap each crisis with the grace of a gazelle, but the important thing is to get over it, leave it behind, and move on to the next one.

Team Events—How well do you work with other Christians? Do you hog the ball and take all the shots? Do you hand off the baton when you're supposed to? Do you do your share, or do others need to compensate because you're lazy or out of shape?

Freestyle Swimming—Have you developed a style that's all yours, based on what God has given you? Or are you still trying to be someone else or follow the crowd?

Weightlifting—Do you deal with "weighty" obligations and responsibilities (like "lifting up" others in prayer and bearing one another's burdens)? When you can't handle it all yourself, are you wise enough to ask God and others for help?

The Long Jump—Do you ever take "leaps of faith?" Sometimes believing in God seems purely logical, but other times you have to trust Him without knowing the outcome. Do you know Him well enough to do that?

Diving—Are you throwing yourself into serving God, or just tiptoeing around the edge of the pool? God is hiring now, not just someday when you get older.

Wrestling—Do you fight temptation, even if it means working up a sweat? Or do you let those little angers, envies, and fantasies pin you to the mat?

Give Peace a Chance

Concluding his letter to the Philippians, Paul appeals for peace: outward peace between two strong-willed church members, inner peace in the face of anxiety, and the peace and contentment that come from the assurance that God will meet all His children's needs.

Before the session, cut apart the role play situations on the reproducible sheet, "Fighting Words." Let pairs of kids draw the roles and act them out, being sure to work in the four words listed for each skit. See whether the rest of the group can guess what the four words were. When role plays are finished, discuss: **How should each situation have been handled? How could this conflict have been avoided completely? What are some words that help prevent fights rather than cause them?**

DATE I USED THIS SESSION __2-19-95__ GROUP I USED IT WITH __Gina, Mike__

NOTES FOR NEXT TIME_____

1. Have you ever had a big fight with someone over a problem that seemed small later? Give an example.

2. The Philippian church apparently had a feud going between two of its female members (vss. 1-3). **What can we learn from Paul's approach to it?** (He could have side-stepped the issue, but he didn't. Nor did he take sides. He told the women to work out their problems and the others to help them.)

3. What issues could cause disagreements in our group? How could people express those disagreements without fighting? (Have a suggestion box; talk directly to the person involved instead of criticizing the person to other people; talk and pray together as a group, etc.)

4. Long before Bobby McFerrin was around, the Apostle Paul was telling people, "Don't worry; be happy" (see vss. 4-6). Other than singing hymns in church, what are some ways for you to "rejoice in the Lord"?

5. How could you "let your gentleness be evident to all" (v. 5) if you were the principal of your school? If you were a janitor at your school?

6. Right now, at this very moment, what are three things you are worried about? Based on verses 6 and 7, how can you get rid of your worry? (Thank God for the many things that are right about our lives; tell Him about our concerns and ask specifically for what we want; believe that He will take care of us, etc.)

7. Have you ever felt "peace . . . which transcends all understanding"? What happened?

8. Look at verse 8. What are the opposites of true, noble, right, pure, lovely, admirable, excellent, and praiseworthy? (Possibilities: false, tacky, wrong, polluted, ugly, repulsive, shoddy, and contemptible.) Which list better fits the TV shows, videos, or movies you saw last week? Why? Which list is easier to "think about"? Why?

9. Paul was so sure that he'd been a good example that he told people to do what he *did* as well as what he *said* (vs. 9). What would happen if all the members of your family acted just as you do at the following times: (a) when it's time to get up in the morning; (b) when you come home after a bad day at school; (c) when you wish somebody would say, "I love you"?

10. What was Paul's secret of being content in any situation (vss. 11, 12)? (Maybe it's verse 13—knowing that Christ, not money, enables you to do anything.) **When have you felt most content? Did it have anything to do with money?**

11. Paul assured his readers that their generosity would be "credited to [their] account" (vs. 17). **If you added up all the money you've given to the Lord's work, would your "account" be small, medium, or large? Do you think the rewards of giving come in this life or in the next?** (We can look forward to heavenly rewards, but many people also find great satisfaction now in helping others. When we give to meet the needs of others, God will be sure our own needs are met [vss. 18-20].)

Option 1: Bring pictures of the missionaries your church supports. After discussing the Philippians' concern for Paul's needs, hold up the pictures. See how much kids can tell you about the missionaries' names, locations, families, needs, etc. Make sure you know the answers to these questions, too. If possible, dust off some recent missionary prayer letters; have small groups scan them and report needs to the rest of the group. Take an offering to meet some of these needs, and/or have kids write friendly, supportive letters to some of the missionaries. *Option 2:* To help kids keep worries under control this week, memorize as a group one or two of the following verses from this chapter: 4, 7, 8, 13, 19.

FIGHTING WORDS

Cut apart these role plays and have pairs of kids act them out. Let skits last for about a minute each. See whether your audience can guess the four secret "fighting words" in each skit.

SKIT 1: SUPER BOWL SKIRMISH

The situation:
You're watching the Super Bowl on TV. Each of you is cheering for a different team. It's a close game. Each of you starts talking about how your team is the best, and how anyone who supports the opposing team doesn't know anything about football.

You must work the following words into your skit:
Nitwit, garbanzo, dandruff, baloney

SKIT 2: DYING FOR ATTENTION

The situation:
A cute new person of the opposite sex has come to this group for the first time. Two of you are competing for his/her attention. Pick out someone to play the visitor, and try to get him/her to notice you instead of noticing the person who is your competition.

You must work the following words into your skit:
Shampoo, airhead, lunch, telephone

SKIT 3: COMMITTEE CATASTROPHE

The situation:
You're holding a planning meeting for this group. One of you wants more fun and games to bring in more people. The other person wants more spiritual depth to strengthen kids who come regularly. You're both trying to recruit support from others in the group. The "let's get serious" person has just said, "I don't think you understand what this group is all about."

You must work the following words into your skit:
King, Bible, potato, cancel

The First Shall Be . . . First

Writing to a church beset by false teachers, Paul instructs the Colossians to stay faithful. He affirms his support and encourages them to keep growing. He reminds them of the superiority of Jesus, and of his own persistent devotion to the Gospel.

(Needed: Marshmallows and toothpicks [optional])

Option 1: If your kids are dressed for it, have them climb on each other to build a pyramid. *Option 2:* Form teams. Give them plenty of marshmallows and toothpicks. Have them race to make the tallest pyramids or towers they can. Then explain that in this chapter Paul emphasizes that Jesus is the very top, the highest over everyone and everything.

DATE I USED THIS SESSION _____ GROUP I USED IT WITH _____

NOTES FOR NEXT TIME _____

_____

_____

1. As Paul began his letter to the Colossians, he called them "holy and faithful" (vs. 2). If he were writing our church (or youth group), what two descriptive words do you think he would use?

2. Paul also said he had heard of their faith and love (vss. 3-8). What do you think people in our area have heard about our church? About our group? About you?

3. Verse 6 says, "All over the world this Gospel is bearing fruit and growing." How do you think Paul and the Colossians felt about that? (Excited, encouraged, as if Christianity were going to be more than a persecuted minority someday.) When you hear about what's going on with Christians in other places, do you feel (a) bored, (b) guilty, (c) glad, or (d) something else? Why?

4. It was the faithfulness of the Colossian people that got Paul to pray (vs. 9). Are you more likely to pray for people when you see that they're doing OK, or when you see them having problems? What needs might people in our group have, even if they seem to be fine? How could you pray for them?

5. On a scale of 1 ("nothing going on here") to 10 ("growing like crazy"), how would you evaluate yourself in each of the following areas (vss. 9-12)? In areas where you're a 5 or below, how could this group help you improve?
- **Knowledge of God's will**
- **Spiritual wisdom and understanding**
- **A life worthy of the Lord that pleases Him in every way**
- **Bearing fruit in every good work**
- **Growing in the knowledge of God**
- **Being strengthened with all power**
- **Joyfully giving thanks to the Father**

6. If you're a Christian, how do you really feel about having "redemption, the forgiveness of sins" (vss. 13, 14)? What's one thing you could do every day to keep yourself from taking this forgiveness for granted? (Thank God for it; confess sins and ask forgiveness; think about kids who don't have it; tell someone else how to be forgiven, etc.)

7. Paul knew and cared what was going on in the Colossians' lives; he prayed for them. Does anybody keep track of how you're doing spiritually? Would you want someone to? Why or why not? (Point out that caring and accountability are important, and plan to arrange for "prayer partners" if kids would like them.)

8. What titles and credits for Jesus does Paul list in verses 15-20? (Jesus is the image of God the Father, the firstborn, the Creator, the foremost of all things, the Head of the church, the first to conquer death, possessor of the fullness of God, reconciler between mankind and God.) If you designed a "logo" to go with each title, what would it look like?

9. Paul's advice is to "continue in [the] faith, established and firm" (vs. 23). Which of the following might make that hardest for you to do: (a) the sudden death of a close relative; (b) moving to another town where you have no Christian friends; or (c) just being too busy to read the Bible or pray? Why?

10. Paul was imprisoned for telling about Jesus, yet he was filled with excitement about his work (vss. 24-29). When have you felt most excited about belonging to Jesus? What things tend to take away that excitement? Of all the people you know, who seems most excited about being a Christian? Do you know why?

The reproducible sheet, "King Ralph?" will help kids evaluate Jesus' supremacy in various areas of their lives. After they display their art work, spend some time imagining what *could be* if they allowed Jesus to have more control. Then encourage kids to pray silently about one "kingdom" of their lives.

King Ralph?

By title and by right, Jesus is king over the world and everything in it. Yet we don't always let Him rule. We sometimes replace Him with other adults, friends—or ourselves. For each of the following areas of your life, we've provided a crown. Under each crown, draw the person who wears it—the one to whom you tend to give control in that area. Be honest. If it's Jesus, great. But if it's you, let's see *your* shining face.

YOUR FAMILY KINGDOM
(How you treat other family members)

THE KINGDOM OF SCHOOL (Who you're trying most to please there)

THE EXTRACURRICULAR KINGDOM (Choices in sports, clubs, band, etc.)

YOUR ENTERTAINMENT KINGDOM (Choice of music, movies, parties)

THE KINGDOM OF YOUR MIND (Who your thoughts would please most)

YOUR RELATIONSHIP KINGDOM (Picking friends, dates, etc.)

THE KINGDOM OF WORK (Job or chores)

THE KINGDOM OF YOUR BODY (Who's in charge of how you treat it)

COLOSSIANS 2

Legends Sleepy And Hollow

Paul desperately wants the Colossians to remain faithful, while others want to mislead them with cleverly deceptive philosophies. He reminds them that Christianity promotes true freedom, not legalistic regulations. And while others can make alternative religions sound authentic, nothing compares to the love of Christ.

Play "To Tell the Truth." Have three people leave the room. When the three return they will describe the same event, but only one of them will tell the truth. For example, they may all describe a visit to Disney World, when only one actually went. Allow group members to question the three volunteers briefly. Then vote by show of hands on which person is telling the truth. Discuss: **How could you tell who was lying—or could you? With so many people telling you what to believe these days, how can you tell who's lying?**

DATE I USED THIS SESSION _____ GROUP I USED IT WITH _____

NOTES FOR NEXT TIME _____

_____

_____

1. If you could get a letter from anyone in the world, who would it be? Why?

2. Paul's letter was intended to build up the people in the churches at Colosse and Laodicea (vs. 1 and also 4:16). Read verses 1-5. If you were trying to resist people who were promoting lies, do you think you would appreciate a letter from Paul? Why? (Paul was always up-front and truthful. Yet he understood exactly what others were going through and could empathize with their feelings.)

3. How can people take you "captive through hollow and deceptive philosophy" (vs. 8)? (Cults mislead people every day. Writers, actors, and musicians influence us. Ads make misleading promises about products. If we aren't careful, we can become the "captive" of any of these things.)

4. What are some of the "hollow and deceptive philoso-phies" you've heard? (Examples: Have a good time, because this is all there is; revenge is sweet; everybody will end up in heaven eventually; winning is everything, etc.) **In your opinion, what's the most "hollow and deceptive" of them?**

5. Why do people fall for these teachings and slogans? (They don't know the truth, so they grab whatever sounds good.) **How can we keep from being misled?** (Vss. 6, 7—Continue to follow Jesus, which includes being grounded in what we believe, strengthening our faith, and giving thanks for all we have.)

6. Is Jesus all we need, or do we also need a list of rules to live by? If we're Christians, can we throw out the Bible and live however we want to? (Jesus is "all we need," but we can't throw out the Bible. Jesus Himself studied and quoted and obeyed the Bible's teachings. These "rules" are a way to help us relate more completely to God; they don't replace a living, vibrant relationship. But some rules and traditions are like circumcision was in Paul's time—an out-ward act to reflect what's supposed to be a more important inner change [vss. 11, 12]. We mustn't be fooled into thinking that following certain rules makes us alive in Christ [vss. 13-23.])

7. **If a person's relationship with Jesus is so important, why are so many religions based on strict rules and rituals?** (Some people like do's and don'ts because they're easier to measure than a growing relationship. Jesus and the Pharisees were usually in conflict over the difference between rules and relationships.)

8. **What will eventually happen to the false teachings of the world?** (Vss. 20-23—They will perish. Jesus, however, will reign eternally. The sooner we shift our thinking from the rules system to a powerful, two-way relationship with the King of Kings, the better off we'll be.)

9. **Which of the following ideas from this chapter might seem like false teachings to some of your friends: (a) Christ is God** (vs. 9)**; (b) Jesus rose from the dead** (vs. 12)**; (c) God forgave the sins of believers because Jesus died on the cross** (vss. 13, 14)**? If you believe these teachings, can you explain why?**

The reproducible sheet, "Lie Detector," will test kids' ability to fend off some hollow and deceptive philosophies. (Quotes are taken from the pamphlet, *The Spirit of Truth and the Spirit of Error,* compiled by Keith L. Brooks and revised by Irvine Robertson, published by Moody Press.) If kids are not able to respond quickly to these heresies, challenge them with Paul's words from verses 2 and 3 to develop such a strong relationship with Christ that they discover "all the treasures of wisdom and knowledge." You may also want in future sessions to take your group through the "Other Religions" unit of *Peer Pressure, Other Religions, and Jobs and Careers* (Hot Topics Youth Electives, David C. Cook) or *When Kids Don't Know the Basics* (First Aid for Youth Groups, David C. Cook).

LIE DETECTOR

Here are some statements that have been made by several religious organizations. How would you answer them?

"In his real nature man is Divine. The inner man is fully Divine."
—*Eastern mysticism*

"The Father [God] has a body of flesh and bones as tangible as man's."
—*Mormonism*

"We believe in intelligent and ignorant spirits. No being is naturally bad— evil always originates in ignorance."
—*Spiritualism*

"Michael the archangel is no other than the only begotten Son of God, now Jesus Christ."
—*Jehovah's Witnesses*

"One sacrifice, however great, is insufficient to pay the debt of sin."
—*Christian Science*

Need help? Look up the following verses and apply them to the appropriate statements above: John 4:24; I Timothy 2:5; Hebrews 1:3, 4; Hebrews 10:10; I John 1:8.

COLOSSIANS 3

New and Improved

Paul teaches that Christians can overcome their old, sinful natures. Jesus gives us power to leave behind our "natural" (that is, sinful) behavior and take on a "new self," with new and improved behavior. This new nature should improve our relationships—both with God and with other people.

(Needed: two sacks of clothes, team prize [optional])

Form two teams. Give each a sack containing more or less the same items of clothing (a hat, extra large pants, big sweatshirt, and socks would work well). At your signal, each team has to dress one team member using everything in the sack. The person being dressed can't help. (If your group is too small for two teams, race against the clock.) Let kids comment on the appearance of the newly dressed kids. Then explain that in this chapter Paul talks about clothing ourselves with things that really change us from the inside out (vss. 12-14).

DATE I USED THIS SESSION _____ GROUP I USED IT WITH _____

NOTES FOR NEXT TIME_____

_____

_____

1. What clubs, organizations, or teams have you joined during your life? What special clothes, pledges, or attitudes were required of you? (Examples: uniforms, haircuts, creeds/mottos, teamwork, etc.)

2. According to verses 1-4, what special way of thinking makes sense for Christians—"members" of Christ? (Because we are "raised with Christ," our hearts and minds are to be where Christ is. We should shift our focus from our own desires and concerns to those of Jesus.)

3. Which of the following are "earthly things," and which are "things above": (a) church pews; (b) your hair; (c) the souls of your friends; (d) pizza; (e) money? (Definitely [c] is one of the "things above," because people's souls are eternal. The other things on the list aren't. But things like money could become more important when used for a "heavenly" cause like praising God or feeding hungry people.) **Does this mean you shouldn't spend time combing your hair? Explain.** (It means you shouldn't *waste* time making your hair look perfect if God has something more important for you to do.)

At this point, pass out copies of the reproducible sheet, "Smart Bomb." Let kids work through it and through verses 5-16, where you'll find the answers. Make sure kids understand what the terms on the "Dirty Dozen" and "Divine Dozen" lists mean.

4. Which three things listed in verses 5-11 would be hardest for most kids to let go of? Why? Which three would be easiest for you to drop?

5. Which three things listed in verses 12-16 seem most "unnatural" for you? Which three have you made the most progress on during the last year?

6. Though Jesus saves us instantly and completely, the changes we make in our lives take time—and determination. Are you closer to the beginning of the transition (a caterpillar or tadpole), or the completion (a butterfly or frog)? Explain.

7. Read verses 12-17. When have you seen one of these qualities in the life of someone in this group? (Get this affirmation process started by describing a time when one or more or your group members exhibited compassion or kindness, etc.)

8. Look at verse 17. Let's say you aren't sure whether it's right to do something or not. How could this verse help you make up your mind? (If you can't do it in the name of Jesus, thanking God for it, it's probably wrong.)

9. Why do you suppose obeying your parents pleases the Lord? (He set up the family structure that way; if parents are obeying Him, they're giving you the right instructions, etc.) On a scale of 1 to 10 (10 highest), how pleased do you think God is with the way you talk to your parents? With the way you listen to them?

10. Do you ever feel like a slave to anyone—a parent, a teacher, a boss, or even a little brother or sister? If so, what do verses 22-25 have to say to you? (Instead of resenting the person, try working even harder than you need to. Do it for the Lord. Let God see that justice is done.)

11. Some people once used verse 22 to "prove" that slavery was OK. How do you feel about that? (Paul's purpose was to tell people how to be Christlike no matter what earthly position (husband, wife, child, slave, master) they had. He wasn't defending slavery.)

Ask: **What's your mind set on** (vs. 2)? **Is it always stuck down here, thinking about the next thing you can do to make yourself look good, or get what you want? Or does it sometimes think about what God's goals for you might be?** Designate one side of the room as "Earth" and the other as "Heaven." Say: **As I read the following list, stand somewhere between "Earth" and "Heaven" to show where your mind usually is on that subject.** Then read, pausing between subjects: **Money; the opposite sex; telling the truth; making friends; your appearance; the environment; your future.** Then discuss as kids are willing.

SMART BOMB

Paul tells us to get rid of the Dirty Dozen—twelve sinful actions and attitudes. But he also tells us to have the Divine Dozen—twelve actions and attitudes that please God. The problem is that these two dozen "characters" are all mixed up below. If you're going to drop a bomb on them, it had better be a "smart" bomb that gets only the Dirty Dozen. Can you check Colossians 3:5-16 and make sure you cross out only the Dirty Dozen?

Pati Ence

Forgi V. Eness

T. "Hank" Fulness

L. O'Ve

Kin D. Ness

Fil T. Hylanguage

Immora L. Ity

Lu S. T.

G. Reed

An G. Er

M. Alice

Hu Mility

I. M. Purity

Evi L'desires

C. O'mpassion

Singi Ng

Wi S. D'om

Gen. T. "Len" Ess

Tea Ching

P. E. Ace

Idola Try

R. Age

S. L. Ander

L. Ying

Who's left? Go back and circle one of the remaining actions or attitudes that you'll work on this week.

COLOSSIANS 4

Visible Means Of Support

Concluding his letter to the Colossians, Paul gives Christians some simple, basic challenges to live by. He also relates specific greetings to and from a number of people, setting an example that more of us need to follow.

Before the session, cut apart the squares on copies of the reproducible sheet, "Square Deal." (You'll be forming teams of two or three; cut up a sheet for each team. It doesn't matter if teams are uneven or if one kid gets more pieces than another.) When the meeting starts, shuffle the pieces and deal them out. Tell each team to assemble three squares of the same size, using all the pieces. That shouldn't be too hard, but here's the catch: Only the tallest person in each group may actually assemble the squares; no one may communicate either verbally or nonverbally; no one may ask for or take a piece unless the person to whom it was dealt hands it to him or her. After one team has assembled its squares, congratulate that team and move to the first question in the Q&A section.

DATE I USED THIS SESSION _____ GROUP I USED IT WITH _____

NOTES FOR NEXT TIME _____

_____

_____

1. **What was the key to succeeding in this task?** (Each contributing his or her part, looking out for what others needed even when they couldn't ask for it, being "watchful" [vs. 2] for what would help the team. Maybe some feel the job would have been easier if they had been "provide[d] . . . with what is right and fair" [vs. 1]!)

2. **Who are your "masters"?** (Parents, bosses, teachers, police, etc.) **What do you wish they would provide you** (vs. 2)**? If you have any younger brothers or sisters, what would be right and fair for you to provide them?** (Love, a good example, guidance, patience, etc.)

vs 1

3. **Paul ties being "watchful" to prayer and thankfulness** (vs. 2)**. What should we be watching for?** (We should watch for the return of Jesus—and pay more attention to the needs of those around us. In later verses, Paul will show he is aware [watchful] of such things.)

vs 2

4. **Paul shared a prayer request in verses 3 and 4. Have you ever prayed that God would help you talk to someone about Him? If so, what happened? If you haven't, why not?**

vs 3+4

5. **How do you feel about sharing your faith? Do you think Paul ever felt the way you do?** (Discuss attitudes toward witnessing. Emphasize Paul's concern for God to "open a door," suggesting that he didn't want to speak to nonreceptive people any more than we do.)

6. **If you had to come up with "Paul's Five-Point Witnessing Plan" based on verses 4-6, what would it be?** (Example: Pray for opportunities to share your faith; act wisely toward non-Christians; make the most of every opportunity to talk; speak graciously and with purpose; be ready to answer questions.)

vs 4-6

7. **How could you make the most of the following opportunities? Find a partner and act out a conversation you might have with the person involved. Make sure you follow Paul's five-point plan.**

• You hear that a good friend's brother was just in a car accident.

• Your history teacher writes on your essay that you've exaggerated Christianity's influence.

• A friend asks you, "Why do you go to a church youth group?"

8. What's the worst that could happen if you told a non-Christian friend what Jesus means to you? Do you think you could live through that? What's the best that could happen? How would you feel if it did?

9. Paul ends his letter with greetings from the people he is with, and he asks about others in Colosse (vss. 7-18). **What can you discover about each person in verses 7-18, including Paul himself?** (Consider charting your findings on chalkboard or newsprint.) **What can we learn from this information?** (That Paul really cared about his co-workers; that when we say, "Paul did this or that," we're talking about support people as well; that there are many ways we can serve besides the more visible roles of pastor or missionary.)

Ask each person to write a note of encouragement to someone who needs it. This could be to a friend, your pastor, or a hurting person in your church. Each note should use as many of these elements from Colossians as appropriate:

Honesty	Affirmation
Encouragement	Good news
Reminders	Challenges
Praise	Thanksgiving
Worship	Personal remarks
Prayer requests	New information
Warnings	Guidelines
Instruction	News about associates

Have kids address the letters if they can, so that you can mail them this week.

SQUARE
D·E·A·L

I THESSALONIANS 1

Walk This Way

Having previously visited Thessalonica, Paul now writes to follow up. He's thankful for reports that the church is standing firm as a model of Christian faith, and he wants to encourage the members to continue with the work they've begun.

Before the session, make a copy of the reproducible sheet, "Original Masterpieces," and cut it to separate the two pictures. When the meeting starts, give kids pens and paper. Seat them in a circle, or at least far enough apart that they can't see each other's papers. Show each picture to a student (the starting kids should be sitting next to each other in the circle), who must draw it from memory. Then let the next person in the circle (on each side) see the first student's version and draw *it* from memory. Continue around the circle, with successive versions of the two pictures moving in opposite directions. When the drawings get back to the first two kids, compare the final versions to the originals. Then discuss distortions that can occur when we imitate "fuzzy" copies rather than the original. In this chapter, Paul commends the Thessalonians for becoming "imitators of us and of the Lord" (vs. 6).

DATE I USED THIS SESSION _____ GROUP I USED IT WITH _____

NOTES FOR NEXT TIME_____

_____

_____

1. Have you ever had someone leave, or perhaps die, before you could say goodbye? How did the hasty departure make you feel? (Explain that the Thessalonians were no doubt glad to hear from Paul. When he'd visited them before, a group of jealous Jewish officials had started a riot; Paul's friends had hastily smuggled him out of town before he was seriously hurt [Acts 17:1-10].)

2. Read verses 2 and 3. If Paul knew you well, what might he commend you for? If this question is hard for you to answer, why is it? (Avoid letting group members be overly critical of themselves. They may not have the same noteworthy qualities mentioned, but they have others. Encourage them to look for little clues that they've grown spiritually.)

3. Also in verses 2 and 3, Paul says faith, love, and hope lead to action. If you had strong faith that God could do anything through you, what project might you tackle first? If you began to feel great love for people who are in nursing homes, what labor might you do? If you remembered every morning that you have eternal life, what school stress might it help you to endure?

4. Paul had said plenty to the Thessalonians, but he hadn't just talked (vss. 5, 6). What do you think would happen to our group if all Christians had to talk 50% less and *do* 50% more? How could that affect your school? The world?

5. Sometimes we think of Paul as rushing from town to town, preaching a sermon or two, and then moving on. But he'd stayed in Thessalonica long enough to show people how to live. How would you feel if Paul were a member of our group for three months? What questions would you want to ask him? What would you want him to show you how to do?

6. Have you moved a lot, or pretty much stayed in one place? How do you think that's affected your relationships with other people? With the church? With God?

7. After you serve as a Christian model for someone else and move on, what's supposed to happen? (Vss. 6, 7—If you've done a good job, those who imitate you should continue to grow. Eventually, they become models for others. Paul couldn't get to every city, but the people who responded to his message spread the Word, and the Gospel eventually saturated that whole area of the world.)

8. Do you ever feel like you're just one person and you can't make a difference? What might Paul say to that? (Paul was just one person in a great big world, yet he was used by God to change thousands of lives in his lifetime—not to mention millions down the ages.)

9. A lot of actors and musicians have press agents to tell everyone how wonderful these famous people are. Do really wonderful people need press agents? Why didn't the Thessalonians need one (vss. 8-10)? On a scale of 1 to 10 (10 highest), how hard do you work to make sure other people think you're wonderful?

Challenge group members to consider what kind of models they are for people around them. Say: **Surprise! You don't realize it, but spies have been watching you every minute of every day for the past week. Their job has been to note your every word and action and to report back to their people what you teach them. The problem is that they take everything you do as an example of what's right. So they might report, "Drinking milk directly from the carton in the refrigerator is good, but only if no one is looking." Or, "A good way to get homework done is to copy from a friend's paper." Get the idea? Now, what lessons have you taught during the last seven days?** Remind kids that even small actions (a sneer, a thank-you note, an encouraging word) may be noticed and have an effect—for good or for bad. Let kids list some examples and discuss them as a group.

ORIGINAL MASTERPIECES

After All I've Done for You

Paul reminds the Thessalonian Christians of how hard he worked when he was with them, and encourages them to carry on their good work in spite of opposition.

(Needed: "Tempting" items)

Before kids arrive, set up as many "temptations" in your meeting place as you can. For example: A tower of children's blocks, just waiting to be knocked over; a tray of cookies with a note that says, "For women's Bible study tomorrow"; a dollar bill lying on the floor; a squirt gun, etc. Watch to see what happens. When the meeting starts, talk about all the things kids *could* have done when they came in, and who chose not to. Use this later when you discuss how Paul wrote that he and his colleagues could have been greedy, could have been flatterers, could have been a burden on the Thessalonians—but chose not to.

DATE I USED THIS SESSION _____ GROUP I USED IT WITH _____

NOTES FOR NEXT TIME _____

_____

_____

1. Look over the chapter quickly. Do you think Paul's attitude is (a) defensive, (b) complaining, (c) happy, (d) proud, or (e) something else? Why?

2. Paul had met some pretty strong resistance in his ministry (vss. 1, 2). How do you think kids at your school would react to an assembly featuring Paul as the speaker?

3. What kind of resistance do you think you'd get if you tried the following: (a) inviting your best non-Christian friend to the next big youth group event; (b) starting an after-school student Bible study on the school grounds; (c) inviting homeless people to the next church potluck? What would you do about the resistance?

4. What sneaky things *could* Paul have done to get the Thessalonians to accept him and his message (vss. 3-6)? (Used doctrinal errors, had impure motives, used tricks and flattery, tried to please people at any cost). **Why didn't he?** (Out of love for God; because God tests our hearts, etc.)

5. Today if you want the public to accept a new product or idea, you might hire an advertising agency. What might have happened if Paul had done something like that when he wanted the world to know about Christianity? (The message might have gotten watered down so that lots of people would accept it. Point out, based on verses 3-6, that Christianity is not just another product or service.)

6. What "hard parts" of Christianity might you want to avoid mentioning when talking to a friend about Jesus? Would that be right? Explain.

7. How could a teacher be a burden to a class? How could a teenager be a burden to a parent? How did Paul keep from being a burden in Thessalonica? (Vss. 6-9—He treated the people gently, not harshly, and did his share of manual labor instead of demanding pay.)

8. What work is done for pay in our church? What work is done for free? If you were being paid minimum wage for your work in the church (don't count showing up at meetings), how much would you have made in the last month? How does that compare to Paul's way of doing things (vs. 9)?

9. Paul says he was holy, righteous, blameless, like a father, encouraging, comforting, and challenging when he was with these people. Does that sound like bragging to you? Why do you think Paul said these things? (Possibilities: To remind people why his words should be taken seriously; to help the new Christians know how to behave toward others; to counteract false teachers who might come along and try to discredit Paul and the Gospel.)

10. Based on verses 13-16, how well do you think you'd fit in at the Thessalonian church? Why?

11. Do you ever feel other people are "hostile . . . in their effort to keep [you] from speaking" about Jesus (vss. 15, 16)? Where do you feel most uncomfortable talking about your faith? Most comfortable?

12. Why did Paul want to get back to Thessalonica (vss. 17-20)? (He thought of the people as a "hope," "joy," "crown," and "glory.") Do you ever miss a person, group, or time in your life that was important in your growth as a Christian? If so, tell us about it.

(Needed: Thank-you cards [optional])

Ask: **Did your Mom wash your clothes last year? Did a teacher explain some formula one more time, just for you? Did a neighbor mow part of your yard because he knew you were coming home late because of soccer practice? If a busy person like Paul can notice and acknowledge the good things others have done, so can we.** The reproducible sheet, "Thanks Return," will help kids list and value a few things that others have done for them. Urge kids to assign dollar amounts to these deeds and gifts, even when it's tough, so that they'll have to think about the value of these things. When they finish, share results. Then pull out a box of thank-you cards (or plain paper) and encourage kids to thank in writing one or more people on their Thanks Returns.

FORM 1077S

Your Name _____

Your Social Security Number

_____

Did You File a Thanks Return Last Year?
❑ Yes   ❑ No

If Not, Why Not? _____

_____

Indicate What Percentage of Your Thanks You'd Like Sent to Each of the Following:

❑ God   _____
❑ Parents   _____
❑ Brothers/Sisters   _____
❑ Other Relatives   _____
❑ Friends   _____
❑ Teachers   _____
❑ Other   _____

Part I ~ THINGS PEOPLE DID FOR YOU IN THE LAST YEAR

Act   *Person Who Did It*   *Value to You (estimate dollar amount)*

1. _____

2. _____

3. _____

Part II ~ NICE THINGS PEOPLE SAID TO YOU IN THE LAST YEAR

Act   *Person Who Did It*   *Value to You (estimate dollar amount)*

1. _____

2. _____

3. _____

Part III ~ THINGS PEOPLE GAVE YOU IN THE LAST YEAR

Act   *Person Who Did It*   *Value to You (estimate dollar amount)*

1. _____

2. _____

3. _____

TOTAL ESTIMATED DOLLAR VALUE _____

Your Signature _____ Date _____

I do hereby affirm that all information provided by me herein is, to the best of my knowledge, truthful—and something to think about.

I THESSALONIANS 3

Where Seldom Is Heard . . .

When Paul is unable to get back to visit the Thessalonians, he sends Timothy to offer them encouragement. Timothy's report of the good spirit there encourages Paul, who expresses his joy because of the faith of the Thessalonian church.

(Needed: Ingredients and utensils for making cookies)

Bring the ingredients for making cookies from scratch, along with a mixing bowl, cookie sheet, etc. Put the supplies in the front of the room and announce that you need the group to make a batch of cookies so that you can all eat them later. Say that you'll be gone for the next five minutes, and you expect the cookies to be ready for the oven when you get back. Don't leave a recipe, but give very vague instructions if you like. Leave the room for three minutes; then return. What's happened? Have kids made a mess? Have they neglected to do anything? Or are they on their way to cookie dough? Discuss the problems kids encountered. Relate this experiment to the concern of Paul in this chapter: that the church he had started and abruptly left would be struggling in his absence.

DATE I USED THIS SESSION _____ GROUP I USED IT WITH _____

NOTES FOR NEXT TIME _____

_____

_____

1. When were you last separated for a long time from someone you loved? How did you feel? How did you keep in touch with the other person(s)? Did you have any fears about what might happen while you were apart? How did it feel to get back together?

2. If you had a girlfriend/boyfriend who was far away, and you could send him or her just one "encouragement package," what would be in it? How is this like what Paul did for the Thessalonians (vss. 1-3)? (Paul was worried about them. He knew they were a young church surrounded by non-Christians. He was so concerned that he sent Timothy—one of his favorite coworkers—to check up on them and provide encouragement.)

3. Paul had warned the Thessalonians that things would get tough, and he had tried to prepare them for it (vss. 4, 5). Yet when it happened, Paul feared they might cave in under pressure. Does this remind you of your parents in any way? If so, what does it tell you about them? (Kids often think parents are too nosy or overprotective, but usually parents' motives are based on love and concern—not distrust.)

4. How has the church prepared you for going through tough times? How has it failed to prepare you? What subjects would you like to see discussed in our group, so that you'll be better prepared for the future?

5. What temptations do you think Paul was worried about (vs. 5)? (Possibilities: Giving up when persecution came; accepting false teachings; being lured away by wanting money, power, sex outside of marriage, etc.) What temptations do you think are most likely to pull kids away from following Jesus these days?

6. If you were away from friends for a long time and didn't hear from them, would you assume you could pick up where you left off? Or would you start to wonder if they cared anymore? How is that like Paul's experience (vss. 6-9)? (Paul was relieved at Timothy's report that the Thessalonians were anxious to see Paul again and still held on to what he'd taught them.)

7. Paul wanted to "supply what is lacking" in the faith of the Thessalonian Christians (vs. 10). How full is your spiritual "gas tank" in each of the following areas: (a) believing that God really cares about you; (b) knowing and understanding what's in the Old Testament; (c) knowing and understanding what's in the New Testament; (d) being able to answer "sticky" questions about things like creation and evolution; and (e) knowing what God wants you to do with the rest of your life?

8. Paul said he wanted the Thessalonians' "love [to] increase and overflow for each other and for everyone else" (vs. 12). Is this realistic—to love everyone? How many people would you say that you love?

9. Look at verse 13. What's going to happen when Jesus comes back? (We'll be in God's presence.) What do you think that will be like? How do you feel about that? If God (in the Person of the Holy Spirit) lives in you now, how do you think He feels in *your* presence?

Paul encouraged the Thessalonians, and was encouraged by their faithfulness. The reproducible sheet, "Encouragement Man," will challenge group members to think about the power of encouragement. Tell kids that they should try to outdo "Faster than a Speeding Bullet" for the motto. As for powers, they can give Encouragement Man any abilities they like—a super-loud voice to say encouraging things through walls, laser-beam eyes to lock onto discouraged people, etc. After giving kids a chance to finish the "comic book cover," discuss the slogans and powers they've come up with. Then ask: **Why does it seem so much easier to put people down than to encourage them?** (We feel inferior to others and try to tear them down; putdowns seem funnier than encouraging words do; clever putdowns get attention; encouragement seems "mushy," and we're embarrassed to show our real feelings, etc.) **What power do *you* have to encourage other people in this group?**

ENCOURAGEMENT MAN

Up in the air! It's a bird. It's a plane. No, it's Encouragement Man! This new superhero's goal is to encourage people—to build them up. Finish the cover of this comic book by writing your responses in the boxes.

Encouragement Man vs.
The Purple Putdown!

ENCOURAGEMENT MAN'S MOTTO:

SEE HIS AMAZING POWERS IN ACTION:

-
-
-
-
-

Sex Appeal

Paul appeals to his readers to remain sexually pure, grow in brotherly love, and maintain a lifestyle that can't be questioned by non-Christians. He puts his comments in the context of the certain return of Jesus.

(Needed: Recorded love songs and variable-speed player; Silly Putty® [optional])

Illustrate the concept of "distorted ideas of love" by doing one or more of the following: (1) Play some popular love songs at the wrong speed. (2) Have kids compete to see who can sing a popular love song fastest. (3) Use Silly Putty® to pick up newspaper illustrations of guy-girl couples, and see who can stretch the putty to make the weirdest-looking faces. Point out that you'll be looking at two views of love in this chapter—one distorted, one not.

DATE I USED THIS SESSION _____ GROUP I USED IT WITH _____

NOTES FOR NEXT TIME _____

_____

_____

1. When you're trying to do something new, would you rather dive in yourself—or have someone there to prod you along? (Examples: Parental reminders to practice the piano; a friend's participation in a new workout program.) **How is Paul "prodding" his readers in verses 1 and 2?** (By urging them to please God more and more, and reminding them that he's already told them how.)

2. Paul says, "It is God's will that you should be sanctified" (vs. 3). **Since it's God's will, it would be good to know what *sanctified* means! Do you?** (It means *set apart*, and is much the same as the word *holy*. God sets apart Christians as His children. We're to set ourselves apart from the sinful practices of the rest of the world.)

3. As soon as Paul mentions being "set apart," he brings up the topic of sexual behavior (vs. 3). **Why do you think that is?** (Sexual standards were very low in the first century in that part of the world. It's *not* because sexual sin is "worse" than other sins.)

4. Research shows little or no difference between the sexual activity of Christian teenagers and that of non-Christians. **Do you find this is true at your school, or is yours an exception?**

5. What are some of the reasons Paul gives for staying sexually pure in our relationships (vss. 3-8)? (Control of one's body shows obedience to God, so sexual activity shows that we have rejected Him; putting sexual pressure on someone else is also unfair to that person; God will punish sin.) **Which reasons do you think would be accepted by most teenagers today?** (Probably just the unfairness of sexual pressure.) **Which would be rejected?** (Probably the rest.)

6. What other reasons can you think of for avoiding sexual activity at this point in your life? (Freedom from guilt and stress in relationships; to avoid all fear of pregnancy, sexual disease, AIDS, etc.)

7. What do you think of when you hear the words "brotherly love" (vss. 9, 10)? If you have a brother in your family, how has he affected your view of what love is?

8. Which movie title best describes the "brotherly love level" in our group: *Nothing in Common*, *Critical Condition*, *Tender Mercies*, or *Fatal Attraction*? Why?

9. Do you think it sounds very "ambitious" "to lead a quiet life, to mind your own business, and to work with your hands"? Why? (Most people in our culture want to lead an exciting life, speak their minds whenever they feel like it, and do as little manual labor as possible.) Why does Paul recommend these things? (They would earn respect for the Thessalonian Christians, and keep them from being a burden to anyone.) If you have career plans, how could your career help draw people to Jesus?

10. Have you ever lost a friend or relative who was a Christian? Who wasn't a Christian? How are people's feelings different in these two situations? (When people who reject God die, their friends and relatives often have no relief for the grief they feel (vss. 13, 14). Because Jesus has risen from the dead, Christians know they have eternal life. They grieve, too, but with hope for the future.)

11. Verses 15-18 are the only place in Scripture where what some call the "rapture" [from the Latin version of the phrase "caught up"] is described so clearly. Do these events sound spectacular? Frightening? Encouraging? How could you "encourage each other with these words"? (Looking forward to the return of Jesus, we develop an eternal perspective rather than a short-term one. Then such things as sexual purity and brotherly love don't seem so hard to achieve.)

The reproducible sheet, "Sex Survey," will help group members express their opinions on sexual behavior and attitudes. Follow with a discussion that's as open as possible. The more willing you are to listen to young people's real feelings, the more willing they will be to hear what you have to say. Pray together if time allows, asking God to speak to each person about any behavior that needs adjusting—especially sexual behavior.

Here's a short survey about the sexual attitudes and practices at your school. Please answer honestly, and add any comments or questions of your own.

TRUE OR FALSE

____ T ____ F   **1.** People who aren't out for sex at my school are classified as "strange"— or worse.

____ T ____ F   **2.** When it comes to sexual activity, you can't really tell the Christians from the non-Christians at my school.

____ T ____ F   **3.** There are a lot worse things you can do than have sex with someone you really like.

____ T ____ F   **4.** I think I would enjoy school a lot more if there weren't so much sexual activity and/or pressure.

____ T ____ F   **5.** Christian schools probably have a whole lot less sex between students than public schools do.

____ T ____ F   **6.** People don't really expect to marry virgins any more.

7. Three words I would use to describe the level of sexual activity among the people at my school are:

8. What is the best thing you've seen happen (over a long period of time) between a sexually active couple? What is the worst thing?

9. Have you or a friend ever been pressured to do more sexually than you felt comfortable doing? How did you feel about that? Do you think it usually feels worse to say no and live with the consequences, or to give in and live with the consequences?

10. What are your main sources of information about:
- Right and wrong sexual conduct?
- Birth control?
- Abortion?
- AIDS and other sexually-transmitted diseases?
- Homosexuality?

11. Does refusing to be sexually active make it hard to fit in at your school? What are the social alternatives for people who just don't want to get involved with sex?

12. Finish the sentence: "To be completely honest, my philosophy about sexual activity is . . ."

Back Without Popular Demand

Paul has mentioned the return of Jesus in every chapter of I Thessalonians. In this final chapter he emphasizes that Christians shouldn't be surprised or caught off guard by Christ's return—and they won't be if they learn to honor God every day.

(Needed: Object to toss; timer with buzzer [optional])

Have your group sit in a circle. Toss around a "hot potato" (any object) while a timer counts off seconds. When the buzzer goes off (or you give a signal), the person holding the "potato" must tell something slightly embarrassing about himself or herself—or the person to the left will have permission to ask him or her any question. Refer to this activity later when you remind kids that when Jesus returns unexpectedly, we need not be embarrassed if we are choosing to be obedient.

DATE I USED THIS SESSION _____ GROUP I USED IT WITH _____

NOTES FOR NEXT TIME _____

_____

_____

1. Has anything ever been stolen from you (or from your family)? How did you feel? What was the worst thing you remember about the experience?

2. What do you think Paul means that Jesus' coming will be "like a thief in the night" (vss. 1, 2)? (Not that He will take anything that isn't His, but rather that it will be sudden and unexpected.)

3. Jesus has given us signs of His coming [Matthew 24], so why is it going to be so unexpected? (As with most of the other things God has said, a large percentage of people will ignore the signs. Some people just don't care.)

4. If the return of Jesus is supposed to be something we look forward to, why is it referred to as "labor pains [of] a pregnant woman" (vs. 3)? (Besides being sudden, it will be a time of judgment on people who have rejected Jesus. And even labor pains are meant to bring forth something good— a new life.)

5. Jesus called Himself the "light of the world" (John 8:12). If you heard that a Christian organization called "The Sons of Light" was meeting in your town, what would you expect its members to do at their meetings? What projects would they take on? How is our group like—and unlike—that?

6. What jobs can you think of that require being "alert and self-controlled" (vs. 6) while on duty? (Lifeguards, baby-sitters, soldiers on guard duty, nurses, astronomers, etc.) What does self-control have to do with being alert? (When on a job, there are always time-wasting things we could choose to do. Self-control helps us keep our minds on what we're supposed to be doing.)

7. Other than sleeping and getting drunk (vs. 7), what two things could distract you most from staying alert for the return of Jesus?

8. Why do you think Paul calls faith and love a breast-plate, and the hope of salvation a helmet (vs. 8)? (They can protect us from the distractions and discouragement that could keep us from staying alert.)

9. How do you feel when you hear the words, "He died for us so that, whether we are awake or asleep, we may live together with Him" (vs. 10)? Do you feel guilty or glad that He died for you? Happy or horrified at the idea of living forever with Christ? Why?

10. Paul wanted people to have a greater respect for those who do God's work (vss. 12, 13). When did you last express appreciation or do something special for your pastor? Your Sunday school teacher(s)? Your youth group leader(s)? If you appreciate something about them, how could you let them know?

11. Look at verses 14 and 15. How could you *lovingly* (a) warn someone who isn't doing his or her share of cleanup work at a youth retreat; (b) encourage someone who feels too shy to speak up in the group; (c) help a new Christian who's going through a drug rehabilitation program; (d) keep a friend from slashing the tires of a car belonging to an unfair teacher?

12. There are nearly a dozen instructions in verses 16 through 28. If you put them in a "To Do" list, which three would you put at the top for doing right away? Which would you want to put off? Why? How might you act on just one of them in the next 24 hours?

The reproducible sheet, "It Could Be Today," will help kids imagine how their behavior might change if they thought of Christ's return more often. Cut apart the situations before the session. Follow the directions at the top of the sheet for using the situations at this point in your meeting. Conclude discussion with a challenge to be ready when Jesus does indeed return.

It Could Be TODAY

Cut apart the situations below and put them in a pile, face down. Ask a volunteer to take one and describe how he or she might respond *without* taking Christ's return into consideration. Ask a second volunteer to suggest how that response might differ if Christ's return *were* taken into account.

Tensions have been high at your school since a racially-motivated fight two weeks ago. You're a member of the school's majority race. Coming to school one morning, you find your locker broken into and paint sprayed all over your books and jacket. A kid from a different race is running away, paint can in his hand, and you think you can catch him.

You would like to invite a non-Christian teacher to your church, but you're a little concerned for your grade if he gets offended.

You are on a date with someone whose parents are getting a divorce, and in his (or her) pain, the person wants to be a lot more intimate than usual.

One of your friends, who once was an excellent model of what a Christian should be, has begun going to all the parties and drinking a lot.

You meet and begin to date the most wonderful person you've ever known. The only problem is, the person is not a Christian.

Vocational tests reveal that you would be equally suited to excel as an advertising executive who can make $200,000 a year selling beer and cigarettes, or as a teacher/missionary to a remote nation.

One of the guys on your school basketball team confides to a friend that he has the HIV virus that causes AIDS. Word gets around, the player is pressured into leaving the team, and some parents demand that the guy be kept from attending school.

Finally, a person you've been interested in for a long time calls you for a date. Your little sister answers the phone and says you're busy for the rest of your life and wouldn't go on a date with this person in a million years.

Noteworthy or Not Worthy?

In his second letter to the Thessalonians, Paul again praises their faithful service to God. He notes their persecution, thanks them for their perseverance, and reminds them that God is still in control. Paul promises to continue to pray for the Thessalonian church, that it would be found worthy of God's calling.

(Needed: Unpopped popcorn, bowls, corn popper, salt, butter [optional])

Bring a jar of unpopped popcorn and a corn popper. Form two teams. Pour half the unpopped kernels into a bowl in front of each team. Say: **You have one minute to pick out all the kernels that won't pop, leaving the good ones in the bowl. Go!** Kids may complain that they can't tell the good ones from the bad ones, but that's fine. After the minute is up, pop the two bowls of popcorn—the same length of time for each bowl. Count the "shy ones" (the kernels that failed to pop) in each bowl; the team with the fewest unpopped kernels wins all the popcorn. When you get to verse 5 in your study, recall how hard it was to know which kernels would turn out to be "worthy." Paul said the Thessalonians would be counted worthy because of their suffering, but not until Jesus returns.

DATE I USED THIS SESSION _____ GROUP I USED IT WITH _____

NOTES FOR NEXT TIME _____

_____

_____

1. Do you ever get tired of greeting people with something like, "Hi! How are you"? What could you say instead? How could you put Paul's greeting (vs. 2) into your own words?

2. Paul told the Thessalonians that "your faith is growing more and more" (vs. 3). If your faith was four feet tall a year ago, how tall is it now?

3. Where in the world do you think Christians are suffering most right now (vs. 4)? Do you feel like boasting about them? What did Paul mean? (The faithfulness of the Thessalonians in spite of persecution made Paul proud of them.)

4. What does the word "worthy" mean to you? Which of the following would you feel worthy to do? (a) become the king or queen of England; (b) teach Spanish in your school; (c) date the most popular person in your class; (d) become a missionary to a faraway country?

5. Paul writes, "You will be counted worthy of the kingdom of God" (vs. 5). But didn't Jesus die because we humans are *unworthy* of a relationship with God? Or does suffering enough make us deserving in God's eyes? (Salvation is by grace alone through faith in Jesus. However, suffering does reveal our character and the depth of our faith. As the Thessalonians endured their hard trials, their "worthiness" [expressing their faith] was brought to light.)

6. Does your "worthiness" usually come shining through in these situations: (a) missing the school bus or having a flat tire; (b) feeling embarrassed by something your dad or mom said in front of your friends; (c) making a costly mistake on the playing field or on a big test? If not, what do people who see you at these times learn about your faith in God?

7. When was the last time something happened that made you wonder whether God really cared about you? How did you work out your feelings?

8. **Doesn't God care whether you suffer? If so, why doesn't He do something about it?** (Vss. 6-10—He *is* doing something about it. Jesus is preparing to return and judge those who have rejected Him and persecuted His people. Until that happens, we should be more concerned with helping people come to Him than in getting revenge.)

9. **Besides punishing the wicked, God will "give relief to you who are troubled"** (vs. 7). **At this point in your life, what kind of relief do you want most from God?** (Examples: Freedom from fear; a better home situation; knowing what college to go to, etc.)

10. **If verses 11 and 12 had been addressed directly to you, how would you feel? What would you do with the note? Why?**

When young people suffer (even if their suffering seems minor to others), it's easy for them to assume God doesn't care—or, worse, that He has brought their problems on them because of their own unworthiness. Let them discover through the reproducible sheet, "How Do You Spell Relief?" that many "worthy" people have suffered—and found God's grace in their suffering. Correct matches: 1 (e, 3); 2 (h, 4); 3 (a[Saul was the boss], 7); 4 (f, 2); 5 (b, 5); 6(c, 6); 7 (d, 8); 8 (g, 1). When you finish discussing their sheets, have kids pair up. Each person should share with the partner a major concern he or she has, exchange phone numbers, and agree to call the other person at least once this week to offer encouragement and see what progress is being made. More people might be willing to stand for God if they didn't feel they were standing alone.

How Do You Spell Relief?

"God is just: He will . . . give relief to you who are troubled." (II Thessalonians 1:6, 7)

Can you match these believers with the problems they faced? For extra bonus points, identify how God gave them relief.

PERSON	PROBLEM	RELIEF
_____ 1. Apostle Paul	a. boss hated this one	1. got a simpler job description
_____ 2. Job	b. really bad skin	2. got a fresh start in the fresh air
_____ 3. King David	c. couldn't have a child	3. God's strength made perfect in his weakness
_____ 4. Noah	d. unwed pregnancy	4. got twice as rich as before
_____ 5. Naaman	e. unspecified physical problem	5. got a good complexion
_____ 6. Hannah	f. spent months cooped up with smelly animals	6. had several kids
_____ 7. Mary (mother of Jesus)	g. restricted by chores	7. got the top job
_____ 8. Mary (of Bethany)	h. lost family and all possessions	8. nations call this person blessed

The Long Arm Of the Lawless

After hearing of false reports sent to the Thessalonians by people trying to mislead them, Paul clarifies some of the facts concerning the return of Jesus. He explains that a "man of lawlessness" will appear before the final day of the Lord. Until that time, Christians should stand firm and hold to the truth.

(Needed: Rope, tablecloth and dishes, or two basketballs [optional])

Demonstrate the concept of "standing firm"—even when surrounded by problems—with one of the following activities: (1) a tug-of-war contest; (2) having kids compete to see whether anyone can pull a tablecloth out from under a few (unbreakable) place settings without disturbing them; or (3) having a contest to see who can balance for the longest time by standing on a couple of basketballs or volleyballs (have "spotters" standing nearby).

DATE I USED THIS SESSION _____ GROUP I USED IT WITH _____

NOTES FOR NEXT TIME _____

_____

_____

1. Have you ever been taken in by a false rumor going around? What were the results? What kind of damage can rumors do?

2. Some people in Thessalonica were going around spreading a rumor: "The day of the Lord has already come, and you missed it. Too bad." (See vss. 1, 2.) **Have you ever heard any rumors about the "end times"?** (From time to time groups of people gather on mountaintops because they think they've figured out exactly when Jesus will return. And there are always books like the best-selling *88 Reasons Why the Rapture Will Occur in 1988.*)

3. When have you been upset by something you've seen on TV news or read in the newspaper? How does that compare with hearing the news that Jesus has already come, and you're still here?

4. How do you think people who *are* left behind when Jesus comes will feel? What can you do about that? (Tell them how to get ready, how to receive Jesus.)

5. Why will many people be deceived by the "man of lawlessness" (vs. 3)? (Vss. 5-12—He will do "counterfeit miracles, signs, and wonders.") **How might you convince a friend during that time that these miracles are Satan's fakes and not from God?** (You'd probably have to help the person know God so that the person could tell the difference.)

6. Based on verse 8, would you say there will be a huge battle between this man and Christ? (No; Christ will defeat him with a mere breath.) **How does this compare to battles between good and evil forces that you've seen in the movies or read about in books?** (In fiction, evil often is at least as strong as good, and the fight between the two is a great struggle. The truth is that God is infinitely more powerful than the devil.)

7. Do you know anyone like the people described in verses 10-12, who would rather fall for a fake than "love the truth and so be saved"? (Examples: Those who are into astrology or cults; those who pretend they'll never die, so that they don't have to worry about heaven or hell; those who prefer human theories to the Bible, etc.)

8. **How could anyone "have delighted in wickedness"** (vs. 12)? **Does this just refer to people like terrorists and serial killers?** (No. Most people have "enjoyed" sin, if only for a little while. Those who don't receive forgiveness through faith in Christ will be condemned.)

9. **To avoid being fooled, Paul challenges Christians to "stand firm and hold to the teachings . . . passed on to you"** (vs. 13-17). **In your opinion, what are the five most important teachings that have been passed on to you? How were they passed on?**

10. **When it comes to your faith, do you ever feel yourself wobbling instead of standing firm? When does this usually happen? How can you build up your spiritual "stand"?** (Know what the Bible says; pray and respond to God; pay attention to church leaders and continue to learn, etc.)

11. **Do verses 16 and 17 sound like things you've heard before in church—maybe in a prayer or benediction? If you'd never heard anything like these verses before, what might be your reaction to them? How would you feel about the person who wrote them to you?**

This chapter tells us what to expect from the "man of lawlessness." But what about us? In what ways are we "lawless"? The reproducible sheet, "Law and Orders," will challenge kids to identify and eliminate "little" acts of lawlessness before they become major problems. Tell kids they must choose one of the three responses to each commandment—no in-between answers allowed. When kids finish, discuss: **Did you wish you could mark some answers "between" the choices you were given? Why? Is it OK to disobey God "just a little bit"? Why or why not? What is it about lawlessness that attracts people?** Affirm the forgiveness God offers for our sins, and give kids a chance to talk to Him silently about their attitudes toward His commands.

LAW ★ and ★ ORDER

Lawlessness sometimes creeps up on us in little ways. We think we're leading pretty decent lives, but we may be slipping a little more from God's standards each day. Here are ten rules you may have heard somewhere before. Read each of these commandments (from Exodus 20) and check the boxes to show how "lawless" or "lawful" you were last week.

1. You shall have no other gods before God.

❑ I worshiped a tree last week.
❑ Something (popularity, getting a good grade, money, etc.) seemed more important to me than obeying God, so I did something wrong to get it.
❑ God got 100% of my loyalty last week.

2. You shall not make for yourself an idol in the form of anything in heaven above or on the earth beneath or in the waters below. You shall not bow down to them or worship them.

❑ I made an idol out of clay and sacrificed a chicken to it.
❑ I spent more time on sports, my girlfriend/boyfriend, or watching TV this week than I did on worshiping, serving, or getting to know God.
❑ I praised God—and only God—more than once last week.

3. You shall not misuse the name of the Lord your God.

❑ I used God's name as a swear word last week.
❑ I misused Christ's name by calling myself a Christian and not living up to it.
❑ I honored God's name with all my words and actions last week.

4. Remember the Sabbath day by keeping it holy.

❑ I got drunk instead of going to church.
❑ I may have gone to church, but I didn't really worship that much.
❑ I really worshiped and rested on the Lord's Day.

5. Honor your father and your mother.

❑ I changed my name and burned down my parents' house last week.
❑ I was rude to my parents, or said something rude about them to someone else.
❑ I showed respect for both my parents in everything I said and did last week.

6. You shall not murder.

❑ I shot my math teacher last week.
❑ I hated somebody, or called someone a vicious name (see Matthew 5: 21, 22).
❑ I showed love to everybody—even enemies—last week.

7. You shall not commit adultery.

❑ I committed adultery.
❑ I spent some time fantasizing about having sex with a specific person (see Matthew 5:27, 28).
❑ I kept my sexual appetite under control last week.

8. You shall not steal.

❑ I shoplifted or stole a car last week.
❑ I copied somebody else's test answers, or "stole" time from my employer by goofing off.
❑ I didn't take anything that wasn't mine.

9. You shall not give false testimony against your neighbor.

❑ I lied on the witness stand at my next-door neighbor's murder trial.
❑ I told a lie, gossiped, or listened to gossip.
❑ I told only the truth last week.

10. You shall not covet your neighbor's house . . . wife . . . or anything that belongs to your neighbor.

❑ I plotted ways to get my neighbor's barbecue grill.
❑ I wanted someone else's looks, possessions, abilities, or status instead of my own.
❑ I was completely satisfied with what God has given me.

II THESSALONIANS 3

Goofing Off

As Paul ends his second letter to the church in Thessalonica, he warns about the dangers of idleness. He also provides guidelines for how to handle people who won't do their share of God's work.

Let four kids have fun performing the skit on the reproducible sheet, "Bill and Ted Home Alone." Then discuss: **How long do you think you could survive if you were "home alone"? What appliances do you know how to use? What would you cook? How clean would the place be after a month? How would you earn money? What percentage of household chores do you think you do?** Note that in this chapter Paul warns against goofing off and letting others do all the work. He goes so far as to say that those who won't work shouldn't get to eat—as Bill and Ted discovered.

DATE I USED THIS SESSION _____ GROUP I USED IT WITH _____

NOTES FOR NEXT TIME _____

_____

_____

1. Have you ever known a lazy person? Why do you think he or she was that way? Did his or her attitude rub off on others, or were others expected to work harder to make up for what the person didn't do? How do you personally feel about lazy people?

2. Do you think Christians are better, worse, or about the same as non-Christians when it comes to being lazy? Why? (Opinions will vary. Point out that there seemed to be a problem with laziness and goofing off ["idleness"] among the Thessalonian Christians.)

3. From the sound of Paul's prayer request for himself (vss. 1, 2), he wasn't planning to be lazy. He wanted the Gospel to spread "rapidly." Why do you think he worked so hard? (He wanted everyone to honor Christ; he knew his time on earth was limited; he really believed in what he was doing, etc.)

4. Paul warns against idleness (vss. 6-15). Why might a Christian think it was OK to goof off? (Jesus might return soon; others should show love by sharing food and housing; it's good to spend a lot of time studying Scripture, etc.)

5. Why does Paul tell people to keep away from idle believers? (The idea wasn't to cut off all contact with lazy Christians, but to make them think and to keep from being affected by them [see vss. 14, 15].) **How do time-wasting people cause others to waste time?** (By getting them into conversations when they should be working, convincing them to do something fun instead of a chore, etc.)

6. Have you ever been on a retreat or at a camp or on a committee where someone just wouldn't do his or her part of the work? How did you and the others feel about this person? How could you apply some of Paul's guidelines to a situation like that?

7. Some adults think teenagers are lazy. Why do you think that is? Generally speaking, do you think adults or teenagers are lazier about the following: (a) keeping their living quarters clean; (b) helping other people; (c) getting to know God better; (d) learning new things; (e) providing for themselves?

8. Do you think verse 10 is too harsh? Why or why not? Should people without incomes be left to starve? (Paul is talking about those who refuse to work, and he's talking to Christians who should know better. Many other Bible passages talk about meeting the needs of the poor and hungry.)

9. What are "busybodies" (vs. 11)? (People who go beyond idleness and interfere with what others are doing.) **How do busybodies spend their time?** (On gossip, giving unwanted advice, asking too many questions, etc.) **How might a teenage busybody keep another Christian teenager from doing what God wants?** (Wasting the person's time; questioning whether going on that mission trip is a good idea; hurting relationships by spreading rumors, etc.)

10. Have you ever gotten tired of doing what's right? What did you do? What makes you most "tired" about being a Christian? (Examples: Keeping up with prayer and Bible study, responding to the needs of others; going to church; turning the other cheek; doing what's right, yet getting less "reward" than those who do wrong, etc.) **What encouragement does Paul give you in this chapter?** (See vss. 3-5, 16.)

Say: **Some things you enjoy so much that you do them as quickly and as often as possible. Others don't excite you so much, and you see how slow you can go—or you just sit there and "idle." As I read the following categories, pretend your arm is the needle on a speedometer. Move it from left to right to show how "fast" you usually go with these activities.** Read the following categories, pausing after each: **prayer; Bible study; homework; church attendance; chores; telling others about Jesus; helping people in need.** Check to see if certain categories are weaknesses for everyone. If so, perhaps those are the "idle" areas you most need to address in future meetings.

Bill & Ted Home Alone

Cast: Parents, Bill, Ted

PARENTS: Well, boys, we're off to Australia. Have a good time while we're gone.

BILL: Awesome! We'll take good care of ourselves, parent dudes!

TED: We'll take care of the house, too! Have a bogus trip!

PARENTS: There's plenty of food in the freezer. Bye! *(They exit.)*

BILL: Hey, Ted! We've got the house all to ourselves!

TED: Excellent! *(They play air guitars.)*

BILL: But I'm hungry. Let's have some of that food from the freezer.

TED: Great idea! *(They pretend to open a freezer.)* Look, there's some frozen stuff! *(They take it out.)*

BILL: But we can't eat this, dude. It's too cold and hard. *(They pretend to hit themselves on the head with frozen food.)* Ow! What do we do now?

TED: I don't know, man. Mom always makes the food for us.

BILL: Wait, dude. Doesn't she put it in some kind of machine to warm it up?

TED: Hey, that's right! Maybe this is it—the thing she puts dirty dishes in. I forget what you call it.

BILL: That's the . . . uh . . . toaster!

TED: Oh, right. We'll leave the frozen stuff in there. *(They pretend to throw the food into the dishwasher.)*

BILL: Excellent! Uh . . . shouldn't it be making a noise or something?

TED: No, dude! You're thinking of the telephone!

BILL: Sorry, dude! *(They pause.)* Is the food ready yet?

TED: Let's take it out and see. *(They do so.)* Oh, bogus! It's still hard as a rock!

BILL: Rock and roll! *(They play air guitars.)*

TED: Hey, that's right! Rock and roll! We can eat a roll instead!

BILL: Excellent! Where are they?

TED: Uh . . . Maybe in this bread box.

BILL: That's not a bread box. It's a shoe box.

TED: We can't eat shoes . . . can we?

BILL: I don't think so, dude.

TED: Oh, bogus, Bill! We don't know where anything is!

BILL: We don't know how anything works!

TED: We don't even know what anything *is*!

BILL: We're gonna starve, dude!

BILL AND TED *(together)*: We're . . . Home Alone! *(They put their hands over their ears, stare straight ahead, and scream.)*

I TIMOTHY 1

A Good, Clean Fight

Paul begins this letter of encouragement and instruction with strong warnings against people who teach false doctrines about God. Then he offers a personal testimony and a challenge for Timothy to "fight the good fight."

(Needed: Prizes [optional])

Have a "worst" contest. Have teams compete to see who can do the worst job of singing a currently popular song; the worst acting in a skit about the worst restaurant in town; the worst cheer for a football team; the worst job of designing clothes, etc. Award prizes if you like. Afterward, point out that Paul called himself the worst of sinners. Ask: **Do you ever feel as if you should have that title? Let's see whether there's hope for you.**

DATE I USED THIS SESSION _3-19-95_ GROUP I USED IT WITH _Adam Gina_

NOTES FOR NEXT TIME _____

1. What if you woke up tomorrow and were suddenly the pastor of our church? What would be the subject of your first sermon? How would you handle your first funeral? (Point out that Timothy, to whom this letter was written, was a young person—we don't know how young—with pastoral responsibilities.)

2. Paul called Timothy "my true son in the faith" (vs. 2). Maybe Paul had led Timothy to believe in Jesus, and had followed up his spiritual development closely. Do you know someone younger whose spiritual growth you could help along? If you did, what three pieces of advice would you want to give that person?

3. Paul warned against spending time on "myths and endless genealogies" (vss. 3, 4). **Why?** (Until we know the important truths and start living them out, we get confused and lose time when we get too involved with the "maybes.") **Based on verses 3-7, which of the following do you think are worth spending time on: (a) Guesses about exactly when Jesus will return; (b) trying to figure out whether Adam had a bellybutton; (c) understanding how God wants us to treat members of our families? Why?**

4. Could anyone else tell whether you have a pure heart, a good conscience, and a sincere faith (vs. 5)? <u>If so, how?</u> How do these things lead to love? (For one thing, it's easier to love people when you aren't trying to use them.)

5. You turn on the TV. A newscaster says, "The top story tonight: All laws in this country have been abolished." What do you think would happen? Are these the same laws Paul is talking about in verse 8? (He was talking about the Old Testament law, but some of our laws today are based on biblical ideas.)

6. If all the laws were abolished, how would your behavior change? *Should* it change? (Vss. 8-11—If we loved God with all our heart, soul, mind, and strength, we would want to obey all the necessary laws anyway. And the law still serves to point out the wrongdoings of those who don't love God.)

7. Which of God's laws do you regularly find hardest to obey? How might a stronger relationship with Jesus help you with this? (Vs. 12—Christ gives us strength, which includes strength to resist temptation.)

8. Do you think Paul ever had a problem obeying the law? (Vss. 12-14—Paul readily admits to the sins of his younger days.) **Why does Paul admit all this?** (As an example of the Lord's mercy, grace, and patience [vss. 12-16].)

9. Do you ever find yourself thinking about wrong things you did a long time ago? How does that make you feel? What can we learn about that from verses 12-17? (It's OK to remember our old sins, but we should always remember the saving power of Jesus.)

10. We're supposed to "fight the good fight" (vs. 18). Who or what are we "fighting"? (We're in a spiritual battle with Satan and his evil forces; we fight our old, sinful natures.) **Does it ever seem like a "good" fight to you? If so, when?**

change wording

11. Have you ever been sailing along, when something caused you to temporarily "shipwreck" your faith (vs. 19)? What happened, and how did you recover?

12. Do you know anyone like the two Paul mentions (vs. 20), who seem to have rejected former beliefs? What does "I have handed [them] over to Satan" mean? (Probably that he'd told them to leave the church, which was thought of as a haven from the devil's power. Satan is given limited power in reference to the disobedient [see I Corinthians 5:5].)

The reproducible sheet, "In This Corner . . . ," identifies some of the "fights" in our spiritual development. After letting volunteers share their responses, explain that we don't need to fight these battles one-on-one. We have Christ, and we have each other. Ask kids to get in groups of two or three and pray about each other's biggest "opponents."

IN THIS CORNER...

"Fight the good fight, holding on to faith and a good conscience" (I Timothy 1:18, 19).

A lot of the Christian life has to do with things like peace, love, and understanding. But sometimes we have to step into the ring and fight some spiritual enemies that will get us down otherwise. Below you will see yourself (a good likeness, don't you think?) and some opponents. Below each one, write in a problem from the list on this page. Also under each opponent, predict the outcome of the next "fight" you'll have with "him." Either you'll win, or the problem will win. The fight can go up to 15 rounds. So you might predict, "I will win by a knockout in the 7th;" or, "If I don't stay in training, he'll flatten me in the 12th."

Opponent: _____
Outcome: _____
_____

Opponent: _____
Outcome: _____
_____

Opponent: _____
Outcome: _____
_____

Opponent: _____
Outcome: _____
_____

Opponent: _____
Outcome: _____
_____

Possible opponents:
Losing my temper in an argument at home • Pressure to drink or use drugs
Wanting to look at a magazine or video that I shouldn't see • Giving up on this whole Christianity thing
Sexual temptation or pressure • Judging other people who aren't like me
Feeling like there's no time to think about stuff like prayer and Bible reading • Using all my money on myself
Being jealous of people who seem better off than I am • Letting my mind wander all over the place in church
Wanting to eat something that I shouldn't • Cheating for grades or to win a game
Starting a fight at school

I TIMOTHY 2

It's Lonely at the Top

Paul continues his letter to Timothy with a plea to respect people in authority. He also provides instructions about appropriate worship behavior for men and women.

Let kids use the reproducible sheet, "Dream Date," to describe their idea of the perfect guy or girl. After a few minutes, give kids a chance to display and explain their artwork and answers. Then point out that in this chapter Paul lists some of *his* ideals for men and women (vss. 8-10).

DATE I USED THIS SESSION _____ GROUP I USED IT WITH _____

NOTES FOR NEXT TIME _____

_____

_____

1. Tell what happened when you had a run-in with one of the following "authority figures": a teacher; a principal; a police officer; a coach; a boss. How did you feel during the confrontation? How did you feel afterward?

2. In order from most to least, how much respect do you have for the following authorities: teachers; U.S. senators; mall security guards; the queen of England; police officers; parents; medical doctors; pastors? Explain.

3. How well do you live up to Paul's instructions (vss. 1, 2) on what to do for those in authority? How often do you pray for those who are in authority? Are you truly thankful for political leaders, bosses, teachers, parents, etc.? Why or why not?

4. The people who got this letter were being persecuted by the authorities. How do you think they felt when they read verses 1 and 2?

5. When Christians are able to have a positive effect on people with decision-making power, God is pleased (vss. 3-7). Yet we're also to "live peaceful and quiet lives in all godliness and holiness" (vs. 2). Keeping that in mind, what do you think of the following ways of influencing others:
- Signed petitions asking for changes to be made?
- Organized boycotts of products advertised on shows that portray sex or violence?
- Nonviolent picketing of stores that sell pornography?
- Defacing the walls and windows of abortion clinics?
- Letters to the editor of the newspaper to express Christian concern?
- Breaking laws you don't believe in so you can go to jail and get publicity for your cause?

6. Do you think of praying as a "manly" thing to do (see vs. 8)? Why or why not? If your job was to convince guys that praying is for "real men," how would you do it?

7. What was Paul telling men to do in verse 8? (To make sure they've straightened things out with other people before praying; to leave things up to God "without anger or disputing.") **Do you think this is harder for guys than for girls? Explain.**

8. **Based on verses 9 and 10, what do you think Paul would say about the clothes and hairstyles our group is wearing today? What was his point here?** (Godly women are more concerned with their attitudes and actions than with their wardrobe and makeup.)

9. **For girls and guys: How could you measure how well you follow Paul's intention in verses 9 and 10? Time spent in front of the mirror? Dollars spent on clothes?**

10. **Verses 11-15 have caused a lot of debate among Christians over the years. Some people say these instructions were only for that local church or for the culture of Paul's day. Others say no, that these rules are still in effect for today's Christian women. What do you think?** (Let kids state their opinions. Discuss your church's stand on this issue, and some of the history of how you reached your position. As controversial as this can be, few will question the main intent of the passage: to learn in submission to God [vs. 11].)

11. **What is verse 15 saying? That women get to heaven by having babies?** (Scholars don't agree on what this means. Having children isn't a requirement for being saved [see John 3:16], so it's probably a good idea to concentrate on the need for faith, love, holiness, and propriety.)

12. **Which of the following instructions in this chapter is hardest for you to follow: (a) praying for those who are in authority over you; (b) living peacefully and quietly; or (c) putting more energy into good deeds than into the way you look?**

Get your group members started praying for those in authority. Together, list some of the authority figures in their lives (by name, if possible) and some specifics to pray for. Then spend some time in prayer for the authorities in your church, in their schools, at home, and in your community.

DREAM D·A·T·E

*A*t last—your chance to create the ideal guy (or girl)! Give this person all the ingredients you'd want in a date. Go for it now—it's probably the only time you'll ever meet such a perfect person. Draw in features and clothes, and follow the rest of the instructions, too.

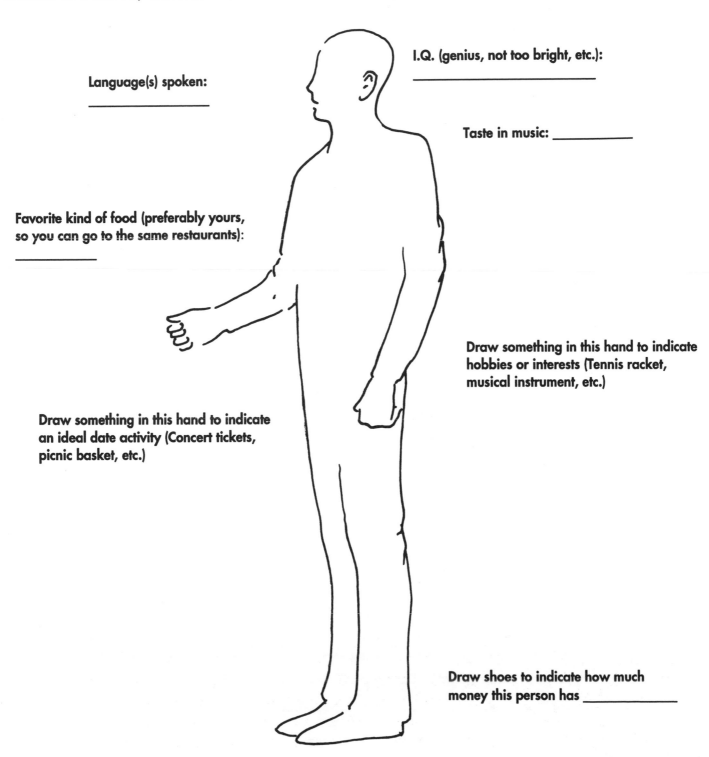

Language(s) spoken:
_____

I.Q. (genius, not too bright, etc.):
_____

Taste in music: _____

Favorite kind of food (preferably yours, so you can go to the same restaurants):
_____

Draw something in this hand to indicate hobbies or interests (Tennis racket, musical instrument, etc.)

Draw something in this hand to indicate an ideal date activity (Concert tickets, picnic basket, etc.)

Draw shoes to indicate how much money this person has _____

Follow the Leaders

Paul provides a list of characteristics necessary for overseeing the church. He ends this section by reminding Timothy of the greatness of Jesus, the reason these churches exist in the first place.

Form small groups. Have each group put together a skit to demonstrate how your youth program would change if you had a different leader. Some of the "new" leaders might include a celebrity pro wrestler, a famous feminist, a rock star, a children's TV show host, or others known to your kids. Skits should reveal—hopefully with some humor and insight—that real spiritual leadership requires certain gifts and skills.

DATE I USED THIS SESSION _4-2-95_ GROUP I USED IT WITH _Michael, Adam,_

NOTES FOR NEXT TIME_____

_____

_____

1. What recent "religious scandals" can you recall? What happens when a prominent pastor or church official is caught doing something wrong? (Church leaders like Jim Bakker and Jimmy Swaggart became "household names" for a while, but for the wrong reasons. They were the subjects of jokes while their ministries were more or less destroyed. Their reputations—and God's—suffered.)

2. What kind of church leader do you think you'd make? What job in the church do you think you're best suited for?

3. Of all the requirements listed in verses 1-3, which fit you? Which do you think would be hardest to maintain?

4. When do people begin to develop each of these characteristics—as they fill out job applications for "Senior Pastor," or sometime before? Be specific. (Drinking habits begin during the teenage years, or even earlier; self-control can begin when kids are toddlers; ability to teach can be developed by older kids who work with younger brothers, sisters, or kids at church, etc.)

5. If you're the son or daughter of a church leader, how do you feel about that? Do family members of church leaders have special responsibilities (vss. 4, 5)? How could you affect your parents' ability to lead?

6. If you were a "new convert," how would you react to what Paul says in verse 6? Can you explain why this could be a good rule? (Paul's guideline is for the good of the new believer as well as the church. The first years of Christianity sometimes contain pressures—spiritual highs and lows, as well as temptations. And most new Christians don't have a background in the Bible.)

7. Why do you think church leaders need "a good reputation with outsiders" (vs. 7)? Isn't running the church a tough enough job? (They must never forget that the church is to proclaim the Gospel of Jesus to those "outside.") **On a scale of 1 to 10 (10 highest), how good do you think your reputation is with non-Christians who know you? How can you tell?**

8. Deacons (vss. 8-13) need pretty much the same qualifications as elders (overseers). How could your dating choices now, and possible marriage later, affect your ability to serve in this kind of position? (The spouse of a church leader can either help or hurt the person's ministry. For example, if your spouse can't keep a secret, people may hesitate to come to you for help or confide in you.)

9. After reading the first 13 verses in this chapter, which of these reactions is most like yours? Why?

> • I'm not a church leader, so this has nothing to do with me.
>
> • It sounds too tough to be a leader, so I'll never want to do it.
>
> • Maybe our church leaders deserve more respect, since leadership is hard.
>
> • Paul should be more laid back and forget some of these rules.
>
> • Most of these instructions apply to me, even if I don't have a special position.

10. Why do you think Paul suddenly quit listing qualifications and started talking about Jesus (vss. 14-16)? (Maybe because church leadership must always be centered on Christ; He gives the motivation and power for leadership and service.)

11. Paul is probably quoting a hymn about Jesus in verse 16. What more recent songs might also fit at the end of this chapter? Why?

It's easy to read about the events in verse 16 and gloss over how amazing they are. The reproducible sheet, "The Greatest Mystery," will confront kids with the mysteries contained in that verse. Kids' "solutions" on the sheet may reflect information in the "clues," but some mystery must remain. Help kids see that our faith does include some mysteries that we can't wrap our brains around—because we're the creations, not the Creator. You might want to spend some time thanking God together for His supernatural, "mysterious" love for us.

The GREATEST Mystery

"Beyond all question, the **mystery** of godliness is great . . ." —*I Timothy 3:16*

Something incredible has happened! As the world's greatest detectives, your job is to figure out how these mysterious events could possibly have taken place. All you have to go on are the following clues.

Mystery #1: He [Jesus] appeared in a body . . . (I Timothy 3:16)
How and why would the most powerful Being in the universe appear in a body like yours?
Your clue: John 1:14, 18; 3:16
Your solution:

_____

_____

Mystery #2: [Jesus] was vindicated [proven to be who He claimed] by the Spirit . . . (I Timothy 3:16)
How could an invisible Spirit "testify" that Jesus is the Son of God?
Your clue: John 1:32-34
Your solution: _____

_____

Mystery #3: [Jesus] was seen by angels . . . (I Timothy 3:16)
How could a man who was buried in a tomb be seen by supernatural beings?
Your clue: Matthew 28:2
Your solution:

_____

_____

Mystery #4: [Jesus] was preached among the nations . . . (I Timothy 3:16)
How could people from many different countries hear about a Man who had only a few close followers?
Your clue: Acts 2:1-11
Your solution:

_____

_____

Mystery #5: [Jesus] was believed on in the world . . . (I Timothy 3:16)
Why would so many people believe in a man they couldn't see?
Your clue: Acts 2:37-41; Mark 16:20
Your solution:

_____

_____

Mystery #6: [Jesus] was taken up in glory (I Timothy 3:16)
How could anyone float up into the sky and end up in heaven?
Your clue: Luke 24:50, 51
Your solution:

_____

_____

I TIMOTHY 4

Time to Party— And Produce

Paul warns Timothy to watch out for people who have created a religion based on rules—instead of receiving God's good gifts with an attitude of thanksgiving. He encourages Timothy not to let his youth get in the way of being a good model of all a Christian can be.

(Needed: Party supplies, refreshments)

Before the session, decorate the room with party paraphernalia (streamers, centerpieces, etc.). Before serving refreshments, hand out copies of the reproducible sheet, "Restaurant Review" and have kids rate their favorite foods. Refer to this later when you discuss verses 3 and 4. As you enjoy your refreshments, explain that Christianity isn't supposed to be a sad, dull religion. God gives us gifts and wants us to enjoy them.

DATE I USED THIS SESSION $\underline{4 - 9 - 95}$ GROUP I USED IT WITH _____

NOTES FOR NEXT TIME _____

_____

_____

Q&A

1. **What are some of the practices of non-Christian religions that you find a little unusual?** (Some possibilities: Honoring certain animals, such as "sacred" cows; prayers facing the east; chanting mantras, etc.) **What are some Christian practices that may seem strange to others?** (Celebrating the Lord's Supper, fasting, baptism, etc.)

2. **How do you think most people see Christianity—as banning fun things** (vss. 1-3) **or encouraging thankful enjoyment** (vss. 3-5)? **Which view most describes your experience?**

3. **If nothing God has created is to be rejected, is it OK to use illegal drugs? To eat five pounds of chocolate at a time? To have premarital sex?** (God makes good things, but people misuse them, overuse them, or use them at the wrong time. The fact that God made a certain plant doesn't mean He wants you to smoke it, and the fact that He made certain chemicals doesn't mean you should mix them together and shoot them into your arm. Chocolate is good, but gluttony isn't. Sex is good, but is only to be part of marriage.)

4. **Would you be a "good minister"** (vs. 6) **if you asked someone, "Why don't you come to my youth group's party tonight?"? Why or why not?** (Sure! We may think so much about sacrifice and denial that we miss out on much of the joy God provides. We need to let others know that our God can provide for all their needs—including social needs like fun, food, friendships, etc.)

5. **Other than physical education classes, have you ever been in an exercise program—jogging, weightlifting, or training for sports? What positive results did you get after a few weeks or months? What would a program for spiritual development be like** (vss. 7-10)? **How could it make a difference in your spiritual life?** (Explain that physical exercise [and improvement] is easier to monitor. Yet a toned-up body will only last a lifetime, while a spiritually fit person lives forever.)

6. **What are some ways that older people "look down on" young people** (vs. 12)? (Some common criticisms are fashion, haircuts, slang, etc. But there's often an underlying belief that young people haven't been around long enough to "pay their dues" or be productive members of society. Sometimes this attitude carries into the church.) **How could this group show the adults in our church that kids are worthy of respect, too?** (Adults may think all kids want from church is volleyball and water balloon fights. Paul challenges Timothy [and your kids as well] to prove them wrong by being good examples of spiritual maturity.)

7. **Timothy got involved in his church with public Scripture reading, preaching, and teaching** (vs. 13). **What are some ways you can get more involved in ours?** (Jot down responses for reference later.)

8. **We don't know what Timothy's "gift"** (vs. 14) **was. Maybe it was his exceptional leadership ability while he was still young. What are some of your gifts and abilities from which our church could benefit?** (Jot down responses for reference later.)

9. **If you learned that church people were starting to watch you more regularly** (vss. 15, 16), **how would your behavior change?** (Most of us would either withdraw and stay out of the public eye, or become more dedicated and try to make sure adults caught us doing something worthwhile rather than something goofy. Challenge kids to take the latter option.)

Brainstorm a list of at least twenty constructive things kids can do before they turn twenty-one (learn to play a musical instrument, drive an elderly person to visit the doctor, vote in an election, etc.) Find out whether kids have actually done any of these yet—and why or why not. Then brainstorm ways in which kids can get more involved with your church. Refer to their responses to questions 7 and 8 to get started. These may seem only theoretical to kids, but try to connect any who are willing to serve the church with an appropriate opportunity to do so. Look for similarities among young people's abilities; try to assemble teams who can work together to get more involved in ministry.

Gina –
Work w/ younger children
Clean up

Michael –
Writing get well cards
Pass out papers
Clean up

RESTAURANT REVIEW

"For everything God created is good, and nothing is to be rejected if it is received with thanksgiving, because it is consecrated by the word of God and prayer."　　　(I Timothy 4:4)

OK, so God created everything—including every kind of food. But how good is each of the following? Take a look at this menu and give each item one star ("No way I'm going to eat this") to five stars ("This is so good I could eat a wheelbarrow full").

STARS	FOOD	STARS	FOOD
_____	Pepperoni pizza	_____	Chocolate chip cookies
_____	Liver and onions	_____	Cheese-only pizza
_____	Raisins	_____	Spaghetti
_____	Orange sherbet	_____	Root beer
_____	Sausage pizza	_____	Hot chocolate
_____	Spinach	_____	Mushroom pizza
_____	Applesauce	_____	Milk
_____	Fried clams	_____	Fried pork rinds
_____	Canadian bacon pizza	_____	Hot dogs
_____	Chili (mild)	_____	Stuffed pizza
_____	Chili (hot enough to take the paint off a car)	_____	Tacos
_____	Pancakes	_____	Orange juice
_____	Anchovy pizza	_____	Alfalfa sprouts
_____	Oatmeal	_____	Pizza with olives, bacon, onions, peppers, and shrimp
_____	Tuna sandwich		
_____	Hamburger		
_____	Pineapple-and-ham pizza		
_____	Curly fries		
_____	Sushi (raw fish)		

I TIMOTHY 5

Take Care

Paul gives Timothy practical advice about taking care of widows in the church and the proper treatment of church leaders. He closes this chapter with some personal advice.

Pass out copies of the reproducible sheet, "What's Wrong with This Picture?" Tell kids that they have thirty seconds to find all the things wrong with the picture. Whoever finds the most things will win. When time is up, ask who found what. The correct answer is that *nothing* is wrong with the picture. It may seem that something's wrong, since it's so rare for some kids to treat their elders and peers so kindly—to help, listen, thank, and respect. But the scenes in the picture are based on instructions in this chapter. Discuss: **How much contact do you have with older people from this church (other than your parents) in a week? How many adults (other than parents) in this church do you know? How many would you count as friends?**

DATE I USED THIS SESSION ___4-23-95___ GROUP I USED IT WITH ___Michael, Adam ___

NOTES FOR NEXT TIME___

1. Are there any older people—non-relatives—around whom you feel really comfortable? If so, describe the relationship you have with that person. If not, why not? Why do you think it's hard for younger and older people to get along sometimes?

2. Why do you think Paul wanted to treat older and younger people as family members (vss. 1, 2)? (The church is like God's family; sometimes we're willing to take advantage of non-relatives in ways that we wouldn't consider with family members.)

3. If Timothy didn't treat younger women as sisters, with absolute purity, what problems might it cause? (He might think of them as sex objects instead of people, which would be wrong and would make it difficult to be like a shepherd to them; he might get sexually involved.) **For guys: What might happen if you treated the girls in this group as if they were your sisters, with absolute purity? For girls: What would be your reaction to that?**

4. Which instruction in verses 1 and 2 is hardest for you to follow? Why?

5. It's a responsibility of the church to take care of its widows. But before it becomes a church problem, families are to take care of their own relatives. Are you willing to take care of one or both of your parents if they can't support themselves as they get older? How much help would you be willing to provide? How would this be "putting your religion into practice" (vss. 3, 4)? (Honoring father and mother is more than a feeling. It requires action, and our responsibilities don't end when we graduate from high school or leave home. Also point out verse 8.)

6. A general principle we can learn from Paul's instructions about widows (vss. 3-16) is that we should notice the needs of people around us and take better care of them. How do you feel when you're depressed and someone is sensitive enough to notice and try to pick up your spirits? How could you do the same thing for someone in your family? (Teenagers can't offer a lot of financial support for parents, but most can provide emotional support a lot more often than they do.)

7. **While Paul is on the subject of caring for people, he writes about caring for church leaders (vss. 17-22). What do you think your church would be like if you had no one qualified to preach or teach? What have you done lately to show your appreciation for your church leaders? If nothing, what are some things you can do?** (Cards or letters; verbal expressions of appreciation; plan a Pastor/Teacher Appreciation Day, etc.)

8. **Do you think Paul's instructions to Timothy in verse 23 require us to drink? Do they give permission for us to drink? Why or why not?** (No doubt Timothy was determined to heed all the instructions regarding church leadership, which included avoiding "much wine" [3:8] and "drunkenness" [3:3]. But since he was ill, because water supplies during this time were not always sanitary, and since Christian freedom allowed for it [4:4], Paul prescribed a bit of wine for Timothy's health. This is not the same as social drinking today.)

9. **Do you find verses 24 and 25 encouraging or a little threatening? Why?** (Knowing that both our sins and our good deeds are being noticed, often by others and always by God, can motivate us to be more careful about what we do.) **What kinds of sins are "obvious"? Which "trail behind" us? Why are good deeds more "clear cut" than sins?**

(Needed: Copies of pages from church directory or other church list)

Form small groups. Give each group a copy of a page from your church's directory or another list of people in the congregation. Ask kids to consider how well they know the people on their pages and what the needs of those people might be. Then each group should pray for at least three of the people on its page. Encourage kids to be more in tune to the needs of others all around them—including those who are older or younger.

What's Wrong with This Picture?

I TIMOTHY 6

Put Your Money Where Your Mouth Is

Paul provides rules of behavior between Christian masters and slaves, contrasts the love of money with the attitude of contentment, and wraps up his letter to Timothy with a charge to stay faithful.

Distribute the reproducible sheet, "What's It Worth to You?" and let kids fill it out. When they finish, have some fun discussing their answers. If any choose "Give up your most prized possession," find out what this item is and why it's so precious. Then explain that one main emphasis of this chapter is our attitude toward money.

DATE I USED THIS SESSION _4- 30 -95_ GROUP I USED IT WITH _Gina, Mike, Adam_

NOTES FOR NEXT TIME _____

_____

_____

1. If you'd been an African-American slave during the 1800s, how might you have felt about your master(s)? About heaven? When you hear about slavery now, how do you feel?

2. When Christianity began to spread in the first century, slavery was common. Sometimes both slaves and masters would become Christians. If you'd been a Christian slave with a Christian master in those days, how might you have reacted to Paul's instructions in verses 1, 2?

3. Why do you think Paul didn't tell slaves to rebel against their masters? (To keep from giving non-Christians an excuse to reject the Gospel [vs. 2]. This doesn't mean Paul liked slavery or that he wanted it to continue.)

4. Who is your toughest "master"? How should you treat that boss, parent, teacher, or whoever? (We are to be servants, especially when we are being rewarded.)

5. In a sentence or two, how would you express your attitude toward money?

6. Do you think godliness is ever a way to make money (vss. 3-5)? (God may or may not allow us to prosper financially. We can't expect wealth as part of the "package" of being a Christian. People whose main goal is getting rich will find it hard to make godly choices.)

7. If we don't get big piles of money as a result of living for God, what *do* we get (vss. 6-10)? How is this better than cash? (Contentment—joy in spite of our financial status. If our satisfaction is tied to our bank balance, we never have enough. But when we find contentment in our relationship with God, we can be happy with whatever He gives us.)

8. How have you seen "the love of money" (vs. 10) cause people to "[wander] from the faith" or "[pierce] themselves with many griefs"? (Cheating to make a few extra bucks; hoarding cash and refusing to give, etc.)

9. Do you think your life will be more satisfying if you pursue money or the goals in verse 11? Why? Which do you think you'll end up pursuing? (Explain that this decision will be a "fight" requiring strong faith [vss. 12-16].)

10. Is it impossible for a Christian to be rich (vs. 17)? (*Money* is not the root of evil. *Love* of money is, as well as other improper attitudes toward wealth.)

11. Based on what you know about the following countries, are you rich compared to most of the people there: (a) India; (b) Russia; (c) Japan; (d) Ethiopia? Where do you fit into verses 17-19?

12. In the following situations, would your hope probably be in God or in money (and the things it buys): (a) Next to a gas station, your car makes a loud noise and quits; (b) your car quits in the middle of nowhere; (c) school starts in four days and you have no new clothes; (d) you hear that another country plans to attack yours?

13. If Timothy gave you the commands in verses 17-19, how would you feel? What three things could you do in 24 hours or less to obey?

14. Where are you most likely to hear "godless chatter" and "the opposing ideas of what is falsely called knowledge"? (Maybe TV, radio, fast food places, the mall, etc.) How can you turn away from these things without becoming a hermit? (The point isn't to give up all contact with non-Christians or opposing ideas; it's to reject the false ideas and not waste time on them.)

As a group, consider making a financial commitment to a worthwhile cause—meeting a need in your church, sponsoring a hungry child, supporting an organization that assists the homeless in your area, etc. Challenge kids to be ready to follow through with whatever they commit to.

1. If you had to be away from family and friends for six months, whom would you miss most? How and how often would you keep in touch?

2. Paul and Timothy had worked together, and their parting had been tearful (vss. 1-4). Yet they separated so each could do what God assigned him to do. When you think about the possibility that God might want you to leave family and friends to do something for Him, how do you feel?

3. Who are some of the people who have helped mold you into the person you are—physically, emotionally, intellectually, and spiritually (vs. 5)? How many of these people have you told about their contribution to your life? (It would mean a lot to teachers, church leaders, family members, etc., to hear that they'd had an effect.)

4. What are some of the talents and gifts that you think God may have given you? How have other people's comments led you to think you have these gifts? Have people's comments ever made you wonder whether you have any gifts at all?

5. How can you try to "fan" your gifts "into flame" (vs. 6)? (Examples: We can never be sure God has given us teaching skills unless we try to teach occasionally; if we have musical ability, we need to use it for the good of the church as well as the school.)

6. What are some things you refuse to do in public because you're nervous, scared, or shy? (Examples: Sing; speak; tell other people about Jesus.) **How can you overcome this?** (Vs. 7—By realizing that God provides the power that's necessary. Suggest that group members start speaking up in places where they feel safe and secure, and gradually trust God to move them on from there.)

7. Be honest. Are you ever "ashamed" to admit you're a Christian or talk about God with certain people (vss. 8-12)? Why? Are you satisfied with this, or do you feel you need to be more committed one way or the other? (Many young people who have previously been told by adults what to believe are now developing their own faith. It's not easy, so don't be too hard on anyone who is honest about his or her struggles. Do whatever you can to make the transition to owning and sharing faith a smooth one.)

8. **Paul was in jail when he wrote this, and was killed shortly afterward. If you lost all your spiritual leaders—to prison or death or whatever—and were on your own from now on, do you think your relationship with Jesus would improve or fall apart? Why?** (Vss. 13-18—See if group members are "guarding" their faith [vss. 13, 14]. Are they depending too heavily on you and others to keep them in good standing with God? Would they desert the faith if persecution came?)

9. **How do you think Paul felt as he wrote verse 15?** (Sad, disappointed, betrayed, etc.) **What kinds of experiences leave kids feeling deserted today?** (Parents' divorce; losing a friend or girlfriend or boyfriend; being abandoned by a parent, etc.) **If you felt deserted, what would you hope members of our group would do for you?**

10. **Paul mentions a friend who "refreshed" him and who "was not ashamed of my chains"** (vs. 16). **How do you feel about people who are in prison? How would you go about "refreshing" someone who was in jail?** (Visiting; writing letters; bringing good reading material, etc.)

When it comes to taking a stand, most young people can use less timidity and a lot more power, love, and self-discipline (vs. 7). Cut apart the situations on the reproducible sheet, "Power Drill." Ask a volunteer to draw one and act out how somebody might respond to the situation if he or she had a "spirit of timidity." Then, as a group, discuss how to respond to the same situation in a "spirit of power, of love, and of self-discipline." Discuss the possible results of each response.

POWER DRILL

A non-Christian history teacher is leading a unit on world religions. He keeps referring to "the myth of Jesus' resurrection." At the end of his lecture, he says, "Any comments or questions?"

The leader of a gang is "hitting on" a girl from your youth group. Sometimes he has his "fun" and then leaves the person alone, but this time he's just not letting up.

A new kid comes to school and says he's looking for a youth group in the area. But as soon as you begin to talk, you realize that he's from a group that your church would call a cult.

That really annoying kid in your math class keeps pestering you and won't leave you alone. He keeps trying to talk to you until the teacher says you both have to stay after school.

Your English teacher asks you to help tutor a student who has Down's syndrome. You think you could do it, but you've never been around someone who has Down's syndrome.

You're on a bus, going to a football game. A non-Christian friend is sitting next to you. You've been talking about TV shows you like. Suddenly your friend says, "I'll tell you one show I hate. It's that religious guy who's on Sunday morning. He's got this really fake-looking wig and he's always pretending to heal people. Oops, I forgot. You're religious, right? You probably like that show."

Make Yourself Presentable

Paul instructs Timothy to pass along the truths of the Gospel, to work hard to be presentable to God, to forsake youthful desires, and to resolve arguments.

(Needed: Team prize [optional])

Challenge your group to solve the old "farmer's riddle": A farmer has to transport a chicken, a fox, and a sack of grain across a river. He can carry only one at a time. He can't leave the fox with the chicken (or the chicken will become nuggets) or the chicken with the grain (another appetite problem). Break into teams of four and assign each member one of the characters. (Allow inanimate objects to stand in for the sacks of grain if needed to make the teams come out right.) Make sure the farmer physically carries the others across the river, and that the others stay in character—much clucking, etc. The team to get itself across the river first wins. (The solution: [1] Take the chicken across. [2] Take the fox across and bring back the chicken. [3] Take the grain across. [4] Take the chicken across.) After the game, comment on how hard the farmer had to work. Observe that Paul talks in this chapter about the rewards hard-working farmers, and others, deserve.

DATE I USED THIS SESSION _____ GROUP I USED IT WITH _____

NOTES FOR NEXT TIME_____

_____

_____

1. Have you ever run in (or watched) a relay race during a track meet? What's the key to winning? (Some say it's the quick and sure transfer of the baton from one person to the next.) **How is the Christian life like a relay (vss. 1, 2)?** (Just as Jesus trained His disciples to carry on in His absence, we are to pass on to others the truths of Christianity.)

2. In what ways do you "endure hardship . . . like a good soldier" (vss. 3, 4)? (Examples: Wear the "uniform" of a Christian and stand out from the crowd; drill and "keep watch" while others are relaxing, etc.) **If you find it hard to answer that question, what does that tell you about how well you're pleasing your "commanding officer"?**

3. How does a Christian "compete as an athlete" (vs. 5)? (Examples: Stay in [spiritual] good shape; keep trying to do better and better; know and abide by the rules; run to win.)

4. In what ways is a Christian like a "hardworking farmer" (vs. 6)? (We may do a lot of work [plowing, planting, etc.] before seeing any results; we must trust God to do His part, etc.)

5. Would you rather think of yourself as a soldier, an athlete, or a farmer when it comes to being a Christian? Why?

6. People who oppose God can stop Christians, but they can't stop God's Word from spreading (vss. 8-13). Does that make you feel (a) like a winner, (b) like a powerless pawn, (c) like you don't need to spread the Gospel since God will take care of it, or (d) something else? Why?

7. Some people are all talk (vs. 14). Others are true workers (vs. 15). Did you hear any examples of "godless chatter" (vss. 16-19) last week? (Be ready with an example if possible.)

8. If you had to invent a ceremony in which we could "present [ourselves] to God as [ones] approved, [workers] who [do] not need to be ashamed" (vs. 15), what would it be like?

9. Are you prepared to present yourself to God? If not, what do you need to do first?

10. Think of the items in your home (vss. 20, 21). Which one best symbolizes how useful you are to God right now?

11. Why do you think we are told to "flee" the evil desires of youth (vs. 22) **rather than "sidestep" them?** (It's just too easy to get caught up in drinking, sex, etc. Running is a perfectly acceptable Christian response to temptation. While we run *away* from these things, we should run *toward* righteousness, faith, love, and peace.)

12. Can you think of a time when "foolish and stupid arguments" led to quarrels (vs. 23) **between you and someone you cared about? How might this happen in a church?** (Disagreements over styles of music in worship; over choice of activities in youth group, etc.) 13. **How could opposition and arguing be "the trap of the devil"** (vss. 25, 26)? (The devil hates to see God's people working together, and he tries to destroy our fellowship and our effectiveness in any way possible.)

Identify some of "the evil desires of youth" (vs. 22) by working through the reproducible sheet, "The Fragrance of TEDOY." After kids combine the ingredients they think would be most potent, discuss the reasons young people are so strongly attracted to such things. (Loneliness; desire for popularity; quest for excitement; adolescent hormones, etc.) Encourage kids to try replacing everything they willingly give up (drinking parties, sexual encounters, etc.) with something that's both fun and wholesome (lock-ins, retreats, volleyball games, etc.).

THE FRAGRANCE OF TEDOY

"Giorgio," "Coco," and "Charlie" have come and gone. "Obsession" and "Passion" didn't even get you excited.

Now there's a brand new, irresistible fragrance for guys *and* girls that's making the rounds at your school. It's called "TEDOY" (short for "The Evil Desires Of Youth"). When you apply it, people flood you with attention. Until you wash it off, you're more popular than ever.

What makes TEDOY so powerful? Its ingredients! Unfortunately, they're a secret. Your job is to figure out what might be in TEDOY. What are the ingredients (the evil desires) *you* think are strongest among people your age? Lust, greed, sex, rebellion, drinking, drug use? Come up with a list of ten or so, and then decide which five of these "aromas" would be most irresistible. Write them on the label below, beginning with what you think is most tempting.

The TEDOY marketing staff would like your help with a few questions:
Based on the ingredients, how long-lasting do you suppose the fragrance is?

_____ I think I could wash it off easily (if, say, God were dropping by and I wanted to make myself "presentable.")
_____ It looks like it would fade gradually over time (as I "outgrow" the desires of youth).
_____ I've got a feeling this stuff would really cling to me. It would take some effort to get rid of the smell.

Now, the big question: How likely would you be to buy and use TEDOY?

_____ I would buy a case, because it's likely to sell out quickly.
_____ I would try it to see if it really worked before stocking up.
_____ I would probably buy a bottle, but only use it on very special occasions.
_____ There's no way I would use TEDOY— no matter how popular it becomes.

II TIMOTHY 3

God's Breath

Paul sends Timothy a list of qualities describing people during the "last days," a list that sounds alarmingly like many of us today. Then he contrasts such selfish, rebellious attitudes with the characteristics of a godly life. He also tells what can make the difference—the Word of God—and why.

(Needed: List of commands to read aloud)

Seat everyone in a circle, on chairs. Then give a series of commands which require some kids to move one seat to the right (possibly ending up on the lap of the person already there). For example: "Move right if you're wearing blue." "Move right if you had a quiz this week." Have some fun with this for a while. Then explain that it's time to play the game using some of Paul's ideas. Use verses 2-4 as guidelines: "Move right if you would classify yourself a 'lover of money.'" "Move right if you've boasted about something this week." "Move right if you've disobeyed your parents lately."

DATE I USED THIS SESSION _____ GROUP I USED IT WITH _____

NOTES FOR NEXT TIME _____

_____

_____

Q&A

1. Think of the people you know. What are some specific ways these people fit the descriptions in verses 1-5? (Press for concrete examples in each case. Rather than accepting "They are mean to others" as an answer, keep prodding until you get something equivalent to "Today a group of seniors stuffed two freshmen into the same locker," or "The police confiscated a dozen guns in a surprise search at school last month.")

2. This was Paul's description of people in the "terrible times" of "the last days" (vs. 1). On a scale of 1 to 10 (10 highest), how well does this description fit our town? Our country? How do you feel about that? (It should sadden us to realize that our culture has drifted so far away from God that we fit this profile. It's also a sobering thought to realize that we may not be far from the "end.")

3. Paul tells us to "have nothing to do" with people like this (vs. 5). **Do you think this is possible in today's world? Are you willing to give up your friends who fit those descriptions?** (It must be possible, because these activities were also around during Paul's day, even as he wrote Timothy. But Paul's command to avoid such people refers to those who coldly refuse to change, or even to acknowledge that such behavior is wrong. [See 2:24-26 and 3:6-8.])

4. Paul had done all he could to counteract these influences with his godly life (vss. 10, 11). **What are some ways that you, or our group as a whole, could do the same against the following: (a) child abuse; (b) brutality in movies; (c) loving money above everything else?**

5. Paul doesn't say that you *may* be persecuted if you stand against all these evil things. You *will* be (vss. 12, 13). **How does that make you feel?** (For some young people, it's bad enough to give up [or be left out of] a lot of the ungodly things that are going on. To actively oppose them and be persecuted seems too much to bear. Remind kids that God offers something better—something worth being persecuted for. It's not that He wants us to abstain from all fun and friendship—just the sinful kinds.)

6. What does it mean that Scripture is "God-breathed"? (Other translations say "inspired." The idea is that God was actively, deeply involved in the writing of the Bible, making sure the human authors got things right.) **If God sat next to you and "breathed" some instructions directly into your ear, how would you react? How does that compare with your usual reaction to the idea of reading the Bible?**

7. The Bible can make us "thoroughly equipped for every good work" (vs. 17). What more would you like to know before you'd be ready to do the following: (a) explain to a friend how you became a Christian; (b) mow the lawn for an elderly widow; (c) babysit for a sick neighbor; (d) rescue a drowning man? Does Paul mean that the Bible contains instructions for lawn mowing, babysitting, and first aid? (No. But we often need to be shaped by God's Word before we're even motivated to do these good works.)

8. How might your life be different if you'd never read a word of the Bible? If you'd read the Old Testament but not the New? If you'd read the New Testament but not the Old?

The game on the reproducible sheet, "Scripture Concentration," will help kids see different ways to apply scriptural teaching. Give one cut-apart copy to every pair of kids. Have pairs play "Concentration" by arranging the cards face down, then taking turns turning over two cards to find a match. Make clear that they are not looking for identical cards; they are trying to match a passage (which they must look up and read) with a category (teaching, rebuking, etc.). Have them refer to the key from the sheet if any dispute arises. After the game, discuss how each category could be helpful in their lives. What might they need teaching about? When might they need correction? Challenge kids to a realistic, specific commitment of Scripture reading on their own.

SCRIPTURE CONCENTRATION

TEACHING (New stuff to learn)	**REBUKING** (Pointing out wrong things you're doing)	**CORRECTING** (How to get back on track)	**TRAINING IN RIGHTEOUSNESS** (How to grow and mature)
REBUKING (Pointing out wrong things you're doing)	**CORRECTING** (How to get back on track)	**TRAINING IN RIGHTEOUSNESS** (How to grow and mature)	**TEACHING** (New stuff to learn)
II Timothy 3:16	Colossians 1:15, 16	I Corinthians 5:1	I Corinthians 11:17, 18
Colossians 3:7, 8	II Thessalonians 2:1-3	II Timothy 2:15	Philippians 4:8

KEY: Teaching: II Timothy 3:16; Colossians 1:15, 16; **Rebuking:** I Corinthians 5:1; I Corinthians 11:17, 18; **Correcting:** Colossians 3:7, 8; II Thessalonians 2:1-3; **Training in Righteousness:** II Timothy 2:15; Philippians 4:8

II TIMOTHY 4

Finishing Lines

Paul finishes this last chapter of his last known letter with ringing confidence in God. Days will come when many people forsake the Gospel, yet Paul could look back over his life, knowing he had "fought the good fight" and "finished the race." He encourages Timothy (and us) to do the same, in spite of the opposition we are sure to encounter.

Before the session, cut apart one or more copies of the reproducible sheet, "Moosic to My Ears." When your meeting starts, distribute the pieces randomly to group members, one per person, warning them not to let anyone see theirs. Then turn out the lights (or instruct kids to close their eyes) and have them form groups according to their animals—finding each other only by making their animal's sound. When the three groups have gathered, discuss what it was like to listen only for the sound they wanted to hear. Similarly people with "itchy ears" referred to in this chapter (vss. 3, 4) will ignore the truth and listen only to what they want to hear.

DATE I USED THIS SESSION _____ GROUP I USED IT WITH _____

NOTES FOR NEXT TIME _____

_____

_____

1. What three words do you think you've heard most in sermons? What three would you like to hear more of, and why?

2. Paul charges young Timothy to "preach the Word" (vss. 1, 2). **Without being in a pulpit, how could you "preach" at school, at home, or at church?** (We can tell friends more about Jesus on a one-to-one basis; we can tell what He's doing in our lives, whether in church or elsewhere; we can live a life that models the Gospel.)

3. What are we supposed to "be prepared" for (vs. 2)? **How is this different from the Boy Scout motto?** (The rest of the verse gives a clue. We need to be ready on any occasion—to correct things we see that are wrong, to help people onto the right track, and encourage people.)

4. How "prepared" are you to do the things mentioned in verse 2? **What more do you need to get ready?** (Examples: A better knowledge of Scripture; more age and experience; a good reason, etc. Explain that we're to start where we are, and grow more mature as we go along. We may never get to the point where we feel completely ready.)

5. Which of the following "sound doctrines" (vs. 3) would most kids "not put up with": **(a) the idea that God created the universe; (b) the idea that sexual relations are only for married couples; (c) the idea that Christ is the only way to heaven? What ideas would their "itching ears" rather hear?**

6. Which of the following "myths" (vs. 4) sounds most acceptable to you: **(a) that God doesn't mind if you spend all your money on yourself; (b) that sex outside of marriage is OK if you feel "ready" and it's "safe"; (c) that you can wait to get serious about Christ until you're old and have nothing better to do? What other myths might sound good to the "itching ears" of some Christian kids?**

7. When do you need to "keep your head in all situations" (vs. 5) at home? At school?

8. Paul was killed shortly after he wrote this letter, and he apparently knew his death was near (vs. 6). He was confident that he'd done all he should to receive his reward (vss. 7, 8). Would you be able to say, right now, that you've "fought the good fight . . . finished the race . . . kept the faith"? (Kids need to remember that the course they set while they're young affects where they'll be at the end of the "race." And we never know when the end will come for us.)

9. Paul had relationship problems just as we do. Verses 9-22 list all kinds of things Paul could have used as excuses for not doing God's work (but didn't). Which of these disappointments would have been most discouraging to you? How do you think you would have responded? (Point out Paul's testimony in verses 17 and 18.)

To your young people, the finish line may seem decades away. They need to be challenged to stay on course and make progress even while they're young. Turn your meeting place into an imaginary racetrack and designate different areas as "Just out of the blocks" (not very far along), "Hitting a good pace" (acceptable for this stage of life), and "Picking up speed" (really good progress). Also designate an area for "Out of the running." As you read each of the following disciplines based on II Timothy 4, have kids move to the area that describes their progress:

•Spreading God's Word;
•Encouraging others;
•Personal development: prayer, Bible study, etc.;
•Keeping your head in all situations;
•Enduring hardship.

For each discipline, ask someone fairly far along the track to share things that have helped him or her; as a group, suggest ways to keep on track in that area. After focusing on the running and the commitment, spend time as a group talking about the finish line and the rewards. Invite kids to request specific prayer for their personal challenges.

MOOSIC TO MY EARS

TITUS 1

Pure as the Driven Slush

Titus, converted to Christianity by Paul, is now on his own, establishing churches in Crete. Paul writes to give him some requirements for people who oversee churches and to warn him to watch out for people who claim to know God, yet have impure minds.

Divide your group into two teams and have a tug of war—without the rope. All the players should face the same direction, each holding the hips of the person ahead. Team 1 (the front half of the line) should try to pull the line forward; team 2 (the back half of the line) should try to pull it backward. Explain that Titus, to whom this letter was written, was in the position of trying to lead forward people who resisted his leadership.

DATE I USED THIS SESSION _____ GROUP I USED IT WITH _____

NOTES FOR NEXT TIME _____

_____

_____

Q&A

1. What's the biggest job you've been given to do on your own, with little or no adult supervision? How did you like it? Why? How well did you do?

2. Paul and Titus had apparently introduced Christianity to the island of Crete. Paul had moved on, leaving Titus there to get churches started. Paul was used to doing this kind of work, but it was probably pretty new for Titus—especially working "solo." How do you think you would have felt in his place?

3. If you were Titus, how might you feel after receiving a letter from Paul and reading his greeting (vss. 1-4)?

4. If you had been hanging around Crete during this time, do you think you would have been considered for the position of elder (vss. 5-9)? Suppose age wouldn't have been a factor. Which of the requirements would have been hardest for you? Which might have been your strengths?

5. What if your father were being considered for elder? Would your behavior help him, or disqualify him (vs. 6)? In what other ways might your actions have an effect on someone else? (Little brothers and sisters, or even peers, might be modeling their behavior after ours, etc.)

6. We should encourage people with sound doctrine (vs. 9), the set of basic, biblical truths Christians hold to. Does "doctrine" sound encouraging to you, or boring? Why? How could you use sound doctrine to encourage someone who got a bad grade because he or she refused to cheat? (Remind the person that cheating is like stealing; remind the person of the rewards God has promised, etc.) **How could sound doctrine encourage a kid who feels guilty for cheating in the same class?** (Knowing that God forgives sin [see I John 1:9] could help the person deal with guilt. Biblical commands to make amends could help the person make things right by talking with the teacher.)

7. We're also supposed to refute (prove wrong) those who oppose sound doctrine (vs. 9). Have you ever "refuted" someone like that? How could you refute the idea that

Christians are just weaklings who need to believe in an imaginary savior?

8. Some people were insisting that a man must be circumcised to become a Christian, even though Titus was one of the first Gentile (uncircumcised) church leaders (Galatians 2:3-5). Paul knew they were teaching improper things about Christianity for dishonest profit (vss. 10, 11). Can you think of any ways people might try to use the church to "make a buck" today?

9. Titus had his work cut out for him in Crete (vss. 12-14) because of the nature of the people there. Do you think it was fair for Paul to make such a blanket statement about all the people of Crete? (He was quoting one of their own writers, though he agreed.) **Is it OK for you to make such sweeping statements about people in any group? Why or why not?** (It's dangerous to stereotype people, especially if we're trying to make them look inferior to ourselves. Paul was quoting, and probably would not have used the writer's words himself. Paul's attitude was generally humble; he even called himself the worst sinner of all.)

10. According to verses 15 and 16, if nothing around you seems wholesome or good (pure), what may be your problem? (If a person's mind and conscience are not pure to begin with, it's hard to see anything as pure.)

11. In what ways in the past have you claimed to know God, even though your actions didn't reflect your words? Is this an ongoing problem, or have you pretty much dealt with it by now?

Review verses 15 and 16 again. Cut out and assemble the cube on the reproducible sheet, "On a Roll," and take turns rolling it. The first time a situation comes up, discuss a "corrupt" (selfish or dirty-minded) response. The second time that situation comes up, discuss a pure response.

ON A ROLL

A very cute person (of the opposite sex) transfers to your school and asks for help finding classrooms, making new friends, and so forth.

Cut out and assemble this cube. Then let group members take turns rolling it. The first time a situation comes up, discuss a "corrupt" (selfish or dirty-minded) response. The second time that situation comes up, discuss a pure response.

A math teacher has tried to break the stereotype of teachers as being mean. He even gives a take-home test, trusting you not to use your books. You haven't studied very much, but you really need an A.

One of the school's more popular people (whom you would love to impress) tells a joke to a group of people who seem to think it's really funny. You think it's not only dirty, but kind of stupid as well.

A little kid holding a $50 bill taps you from behind and asks, "Excuse me, did you drop this?" (You didn't.)

As you bow your head to pray over the mystery meat in the school cafeteria, you notice the kids at the next table nudging each other and smirking at you.

Your best friend stops you in the hall and breathlessly exclaims, "You'll never believe what I just heard about so-and-so. . . ."

TITUS 2

Control Yourself

Titus, as the person responsible for establishing church order in Crete, is given instructions for the spiritual development of all age-groups, as well as slaves and masters. To live up to these expectations, self-control becomes a necessary quality.

Play "If you love me, honey, smile." Designate a girl to come up to any guy and say, "If you love me, honey, smile." If the guy can respond, "I love you, honey, but I just can't smile," with a straight face, the girl must try someone else. But if the guy cracks a smile, he becomes "It" and must get a girl to smile. (Note: If you don't have both genders in your group, just have several kids do all they can [without touching] to make a volunteer smile.) Explain that in this chapter Paul calls for even more self-control than it takes not to smile during the game.

DATE I USED THIS SESSION _____ GROUP I USED IT WITH _____

NOTES FOR NEXT TIME _____

_____

_____

1. Not including pastors or "official" church leaders, who is the best example of what you believe a real Christian should be?

2. When you hear the words, "old man," what image comes to mind? How about "old woman"? (Listen for stereotypes, and compare such answers with what Paul says older men [vs. 2] and older women [vs. 3] should be.)

3. What older men and women do you know who meet Paul's criteria?

4. Now look at the goals for younger women (vss. 4, 5). Are these realistic for today's woman? Can a woman have a career, an opinion of her own, and still be subject to her husband (assuming she's married)? (The call for submission by no means suggests that the submissive party is a mindless airhead, completely dependent on the other person. Jesus Himself was submissive to the will of God the Father, while remaining one with Him. Similarly, as wives voluntarily submit to husbands, both can grow stronger spiritually and be good working models for Christian life and marriage.)

5. Paul gives young men only one instruction (vs. 6). Are they off the hook? Explain. (Have group members list the practical applications of self-control: Resist the temptation to go drinking with the guys; eliminate offensive language; treat everyone with respect, even when you don't feel like it; maintain sexual self-control, etc.)

6. Look at verses 6 through 8. What do you think young men today especially need to learn about integrity? (Keeping promises; not taking advantage of young women; respecting the law, etc.) **About seriousness?** (Not spending all their time on entertainment, etc.) **About soundness of speech?** (Meaning what they say; not swearing, etc.) **How do these apply to young women, too?**

7. Paul seems pretty concerned about how our behavior looks to non-Christians (vs. 8). How do you feel about this? Is your attitude closer to (a) "I can't take the chance of offending anybody," or (b) "If people don't like what I do, that's their problem"?

8. How do Paul's instructions to Titus regarding slaves and masters (vss. 9, 10) **apply to our own relationships with employers, teachers, or parents?** (Even if we disagree with them over specifics, we are to respect their positions and subject ourselves to them.)

9. Why should we go out of our way to be so nice and pure (vss. 11-15)? (Our salvation is a gift from God that we didn't deserve. And Jesus will return one day, so we should be watchful. The sacrifices we make for God are nothing in comparison to those He made for us. If we are truly grateful, living up to these guidelines won't be a chore. Rather, we will be "eager to do what is good.")

10. If you were getting started right away to become everything God wants you to be, what's the first thing you would need to start doing? What's the first thing you would need to stop doing?

The word self-control occurs frequently in this chapter (vss. 2, 5, 6, 12), so the reproducible sheet, "Get Control," will allow kids to consider how self-controlled they are. When they finish, discuss as much as they are willing. Explain that developing self-control sometimes is easier when we allow "others-control" as well. That is, if we're accountable to others, we're less likely to forget or slip up. Encourage kids to get in groups of two or three and share areas where they most need additional self-control. Encourage kids to "authorize" each other to follow up on one another, at least during the coming week.

GET CONTROL

Just when we think we're starting to develop self-control, we find ourselves screaming at a parent . . . taking a swing at a player on the other team . . . taking a drink at a party . . . taking a third donut when we're supposed to be dieting . . . or worse. So in each of the areas below:

1 Fill in the Self-Control-O-Meter to show how well you're doing in that area;

2 Identify your strong and weak points in that area;

3 Think about what needs to happen in order for you to show more self-control in that area.

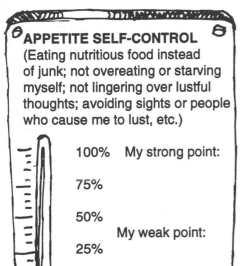

APPETITE SELF-CONTROL
(Eating nutritious food instead of junk; not overeating or starving myself; not lingering over lustful thoughts; avoiding sights or people who cause me to lust, etc.)

100%   My strong point:
75%
50%
         My weak point:
25%
0%

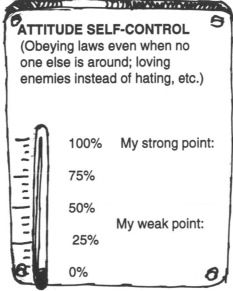

ATTITUDE SELF-CONTROL
(Obeying laws even when no one else is around; loving enemies instead of hating, etc.)

100%   My strong point:
75%
50%
         My weak point:
25%
0%

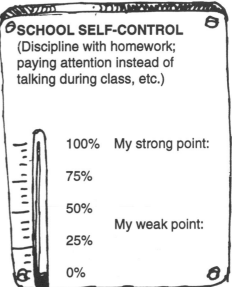

SCHOOL SELF-CONTROL
(Discipline with homework; paying attention instead of talking during class, etc.)

100%   My strong point:
75%
50%
         My weak point:
25%
0%

FAMILY SELF-CONTROL
(Not blowing up at parents or siblings; not demanding my own way; not hogging the phone, etc.)

100%   My strong point:
75%
50%
         My weak point:
25%
0%

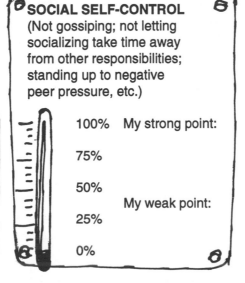

SOCIAL SELF-CONTROL
(Not gossiping; not letting socializing take time away from other responsibilities; standing up to negative peer pressure, etc.)

100%   My strong point:
75%
50%
         My weak point:
25%
0%

WORK SELF-CONTROL
(Doing my best; not goofing off; doing chores without being asked, etc.)

100%   My strong point:
75%
50%
         My weak point:
25%
0%

TITUS 3

Tyrants and Troublemakers

After urging self-control in the previous chapter, Paul ends his letter to Titus with the reminder that we're also to place ourselves under the control of higher authorities. He emphasizes the importance of submission to leaders and the misery of a life not submitted to Christ. He also urges Titus not to let troublemakers take control.

(Needed: Blindfolds; chairs or other obstacles)

Before the session, cut apart the cards on the reproducible sheet, "Crash Course." Divide into two teams of four or more and distribute the cards. Tell kids not to share what's written on their cards. (If you have fewer than eight group members, distribute only the "out of control" cards and race against the clock. If you have more than eight, make extra copies of all but the "Leader" cards.) After letting kids read their cards (privately), blindfold all but the team leaders. Set up a very simple obstacle course, and have the leaders direct their team members through it. The "under control" kids should succeed quickly; let them take off their blindfolds and watch the "out of control" team blunder around. Use this to illustrate our need to submit to authority.

DATE I USED THIS SESSION _____ GROUP I USED IT WITH _____

NOTES FOR NEXT TIME _____

_____

_____

Q&A

1. Who's the best boss or teacher you ever had?

2. But what if you don't get along with someone who has a position of authority over you (vss. 1, 2)? How do you tend to treat that person? How *should* you treat him or her? (As Christians, we are to "be subject to" such people anyway. Paul's instructions were written during the time of the ungodly and often cruel Roman Empire, so we can find little excuse for disobeying today.)

3. Look at verses 1 and 2 again. How can we "be ready to do whatever is good"? (Look for people who need help; *Pray* know how to help; be willing to help, etc.) **What would be your "response time" if you saw someone who (a) had a flat tire; (b) had a "Kick Me" sign taped to his or her back; (c) was being attacked in a deserted school playground?**

4. If being peaceable toward others were measured in pounds, how heavy would your "peaceability" be? If being considerate were measured in dollars, how much would you have in your wallet or purse right now? If humility were measured in miles, how far have you gone in the last year?

5. Christians don't stop being people. They still have most of the same feelings, problems, emotions, and desires as non-Christians. So how can we suddenly start living by another, higher, set of guidelines (vss. 3-8)? (When you become a Christian, God's mercy and salvation [vs. 5] make possible a "washing of rebirth and renewal by the Holy Spirit." We can't simply decide to live according to higher standards. The power to do so must come from God.)

6. Even with God's power, "doing what is good" takes effort (vs. 8). Can you think of anything you saw on TV last week that reflected an old, rebellious nature (vs. 3) more than a new relationship in Christ? (Look for specific instances of disobedience, deception, enslavement by pleasure, malice, envy, hatred, etc.) **Which seems more interesting—the old nature or the new? Why do you think that is?**

7. Paul challenges Titus (and us) to spread the word about the change God can make in a person's life. Have you "stressed" these things to anyone (vs. 8)? If so, what happened? Or is it more accurate to say that you mention these things to just a few people every once in a while? Or that you hardly even think about them yourself?

8. God doesn't want us wasting our time if people don't want to listen. What are you supposed to do if you come upon a "divisive person" as you try to maintain a pure Christian life (vss. 9-11)? (We are to avoid getting tangled up in arguments with people who only want to prove us wrong, not really discuss. After a couple of warnings, we are to "have nothing to do with" such people and move on.)

9. What if some of these divisive people are those you really care about—close friends or family members? (We still have responsibilities to family members. And we can pray for others. Perhaps one day they'll be ready to listen and discuss God's claims. The important thing is not to let such people harm our relationship with God. As long as we remember that God is in control and trust Him to do what we are unable to do, we can be faithful to Him in spite of situations we would prefer to see changed.)

Our lives should change after we experience God's love and power. Distribute paper and pens and ask kids to illustrate some of the differences by using a before-and-after approach as the diet and hair transplant ads do—including symbols that somehow reflect their own actions, priorities, and attitudes. Let them explain their pictures. Then go around the room and let each person say, "One area I'm going to put under God's control this week is _____." If possible, follow up on these commitments at a future meeting.

CRASHCOURSE

"OUT OF CONTROL" TEAM CARDS

LEADER: Your job is to direct your team through the maze—using only your voice.

TROUBLEMAKER: Contradict everything the team leader says.

REBEL: Do the opposite of what others tell you.

REBEL: Do the opposite of what others tell you.

TROUBLEMAKER: Contradict everything the team leader says.

REBEL: Do the opposite of what others tell you.

"UNDER CONTROL" TEAM CARDS

LEADER: Your job is to direct your team through the maze—using only your voice.

TEAM MEMBER: Your team leader will give you good directions; listen and follow them.

TEAM MEMBER: Your team leader will give you good directions; listen and follow them.

TEAM MEMBER: Your team leader will give you good directions; listen and follow them.

TEAM MEMBER: Your team leader will give you good directions; listen and follow them.

TEAM MEMBER: Your team leader will give you good directions; listen and follow them.

PHILEMON

Back to the Ball and Chain

Onesimus, a runaway slave who has stolen from his master, Philemon, meets the apostle Paul and becomes a Christian. Paul then writes this letter, to be carried back by Onesimus, asking Philemon to receive his slave with forgiveness, as a brother.

Play some games requiring strength—arm wrestling, tug of war, etc. At first, make the competition uneven by pitting some of the stronger kids against weaker ones. But after one round, change the rules so the game becomes two-against-one rather than one-against-one. This time team your very strongest people with the weaker ones against their previous opponents. Later, parallel this experience with the story of Philemon: Onesimus felt too weak to return on his own, yet was willing to return as an ally of Paul.

DATE I USED THIS SESSION ___3-12-95___ GROUP I USED IT WITH ___Michael___

NOTES FOR NEXT TIME _____

_____

_____

Q&A

1. Have you ever done anything that you were sorry for, yet never expected the other person(s) to forgive? How did it get resolved—or did it?

2. Put yourself in the place of Onesimus. You've stolen something from your master (Philemon) and then run away, which is punishable by death. While you're "on the lam," you meet Paul and become a Christian. He sends you back, along with a letter to Philemon asking him to take you back. How do you think you would feel? (Nervous, guilty, etc.)

3. Now put yourself in Philemon's place. Your runaway slave shows up, hands you a letter from Paul—yes, *the* Paul—and you read verses 1-7. How would you feel? (Willing to forgive; wanting to get even; wanting to punish, but less harshly, etc.)

4. How do you feel when someone asks you for a favor, telling you what the "right" response would be? When it comes to asking for favors, what can you learn from Paul's appeal to Philemon (vss. 8-10)? (Paul wasn't wishy-washy, but he wasn't overbearing, either. He didn't try to pull strings because of his position in the Christian community, but rather asked a favor, person-to-person.)

5. Paul uses a play on words in verse 11. "Onesimus" meant "useful," but he hadn't lived up to his name. How do people today either succeed or fail to "live up to their names"? (People honor [or dishonor] family names, rally around the name "American," and get excited about school symbols [like the "fighting Irish" of Notre Dame]. **On a scale of 1 to 10 (with 10 highest), how well do you think you live up to the name "Christian"?**

6. How did Paul make it clear that Onesimus was still useful (vss. 12-14)? Have you ever been built up by someone in a similar way? How did you feel?

7. Onesimus left Philemon as a sinful slave and returned as a fellow Christian (vss. 15, 16). The experience probably wasn't pleasant for him, yet it was the best thing that could have happened. Have you (or a friend or family member) ever gone through what seemed to be a horrible experience that turned out for the best? What do you think God's part in that was?

8. Paul put himself on the line for Onesimus after knowing him only a short time (vss. 17, 18), **and even though Paul was a well-known and respected figure in the Christian community** (vss. 19-25). **Have you ever defended someone else? If so, how? How would you decide whether to "put yourself on the line" for someone else? How does that compare with Paul's example?**

9. Do you think Paul was approving slavery by sending Onesimus back? (Nowhere does he say so. He is concerned that Christians obey the existing laws, which required that Philemon's "property" be returned. But he showed that the new Christian-to-Christian bond was far more important than the slave-to-master bond.)

Even with Paul's support, returning to Philemon must have been one of the hardest things Onesimus ever did. The reproducible sheet, "Making It Right," asks your group members to think of one of their conflicts and create a plan to remedy the problem. When they finish, spend a little time as a group discussing why it is so important for Christians to resolve difficult conflicts. Remind them that a person's relationship with God should be the one he or she cares about most. And when we begin to put God first, we start to see how valuable all our other relationships are as well.

Making It Right

At times we all find ourselves in the embarrassing position of Onesimus. We do something wrong, run away, and then live in fear of being caught, reprimanded, expelled, disowned, or grounded. The good news is that God wants us to overcome these fears and get back to a happy, peaceful life. The "bad" news is the way this happens: by swallowing your pride, going back to the person you offended, and making the situation right again.

In the space below, describe a situation you need to get settled—even if it wouldn't be fun to do so. Maybe, like Onesimus, you're a thief. (Have you ever shoplifted an item? "Stolen" time from a boss by goofing off when you were getting paid?) Maybe you have a shaky relationship with someone and you need to take the lead in getting it worked out. Whatever comes to mind, write it below. And then write out a plan to do something about it.

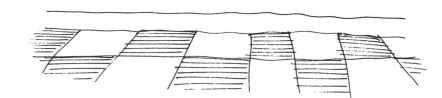

See, here's the problem:

The person(s) I need to apologize to is/are:

The best time to do this would be:

A couple of alternative times are:

___ I'm ready to talk to this person and try to work things out.

___ Like Onesimus, I wish I had someone else's support first. Someone who might be willing to help me is: _____ .

The main thing that has been keeping me from doing this is:

Angel Stadium

The Book of Hebrews is addressed to the Jewish people, who knew of all the appearances of angels found in their Scriptures. Jesus, the Son of God, is superior even to the angels.

(Needed: List of auction items, and perhaps play money)

Conduct an auction. Hand out play money, or just assign kids a sum from which they can deduct the costs of their purchases and keep a running total. Begin with items—both tangible and intangible—that many kids would like (a new Corvette, straight *A's* for a month, $50/week for clothes, etc.). As kids run out of money, start offering better and better items (a new Porsche, straight *A's* for the *year*, ownership of a fashion store, etc.). Then point out that we don't always know when something better is going to come along. This chapter tells the Hebrews (and us) about Someone better than anything, or anyone, that had come along in their whole history.

DATE I USED THIS SESSION _____ GROUP I USED IT WITH _____

NOTES FOR NEXT TIME _____

_____

_____

1. **What's your mental picture of an angel? Where do you get that image?** (Discuss the variety of descriptions: a white glowing creature with huge wings and a halo; an "undercover" heavenly messenger, indistinguishable from a human; the character of Clarence in *It's a Wonderful Life*; other movie treatments in which angels are beautiful young women, etc.)

2. **If an angel appeared right here to give us a personal message from God, would you calm down when he said, "Fear not"? How do you think you would feel after one minute? After one hour?**

3. **If Jesus Himself appeared right here to give us a personal message, how would your reaction compare to the reaction you'd have to an angel? Why?** (We're not to dismiss the significance of angels, God's special messengers. Yet as impressive as angels have been when they've been sent to appear, we are not to give them more attention than we do Jesus.)

4. **In what ways has God "spoken to us by his Son"** (vss. 1, 2)? (Not only when He taught here on earth, but also through the Bible, His Word inspired by His Holy Spirit.)

5. **Verses 2-4 name some ways in which Jesus is better and more important than the angels. Which of these facts about Jesus do you think about most often? Least often? How do they affect your life—or do they?** (If we truly begin to consider the sacrifice Jesus made in light of His position, we must either try to conform to His standards or intentionally reject Him. The better we understand, the less excuse we have when we don't obey and follow Him.)

6. **The writer of Hebrews lists a long series of quotations from the Old Testament that describe the one-of-a-kind nature of Jesus, which sets Him apart from any other supernatural being** (vss. 5-13). **In your opinion, which of the quotes best demonstrates that Jesus is superior to anything else?** (After kids respond, be sure to comment on the Son-Father relationship [vs. 5] between Jesus and God. This is important because through Jesus' sacrificial death we all have the privilege of becoming children of God [I John 3:1].)

7. Do you think angels mind being "ministering spirits sent to serve those who will inherit salvation" (vs. 14)? Explain. (Remember that Satan's original rebellion was over a secondary position in creation, and some of the hosts of heaven have chosen to follow him instead of God [Isaiah 14:12-15; Matthew 25:41]. Yet those who serve God faithfully, including humans who choose to do so, will eventually live together in God's kingdom where there will be no question as to who is #1, and it just won't matter who's #2.)

8. What do you think would be the hardest part about serving human beings (vs. 14)? (Maybe putting up with their imperfections.) When do you think it would it be hardest for an angel to be around you? Why?

9. Do you ever complain about being a servant of God? If so, how? If serving is good enough for angels, why do we sometimes think it's not good enough for us? (Contrast our usual short-term thinking with God's eternal perspective.)

The reproducible sheet, "Pyramid of Priorities," will ask group members to rank the things they value. When they finish, discuss the things they tend to put ahead of Jesus—and why they do so. (Note: Many kids may put Jesus at the top of the diagram because it's "expected." Challenge them to explain *how* they put Him first.) Also be prepared for further questions concerning angels. Answer as many as you can, and consider making this a topic of research for some of your more committed group members. To see how much kids are aware of the ministry of angels, you might want to ask how many biblical appearances of angels they can recall—the people they appeared to and the messages that were delivered.

Pyramid of Priorities

What are your top priorities? Maybe they shift around. Maybe you struggle to know what to put first. For example, should you skip football practice to go to the special youth group outing, risking the full wrath of the coach? Do you baby-sit like your parents want you to, or go out with your friends where you're almost sure to run into that cute person in geometry who has been looking at you with some "angles" of his/her own?

Speaking of geometry, below is a pyramid (OK, it's actually a triangle, but pretend it's three-dimensional) in which you are to record your priorities—right here, right now. First, list the top priorities of your life. Then put them at the appropriate level on the pyramid (most important on the top, and on down—there's room for 15 of them). We've listed a few to get you started.

PRIORITIES

1. My own comfort/pleasure
2. My family
3. My schoolwork/grades
4. Jesus
5. My friends
6. Dating
7. Work
8. Money/possessions
9.
10.
11.
12.
13.
14.
15.

He Ain't Just Heavenly, He's My Brother

We must not ignore God's great message of salvation. The Author of that salvation was made like us, and even calls us brothers.

Play a variation of charades. Kids should try to communicate movie or song titles, but without using their hands. And they *must* speak—but in "nonsense" words, not in any recognizable language. See how much kids can get across under these limitations. Then discuss the problem of communicating between God and people. As you'll see in this chapter, God got His message across in a special way through Christ.

DATE I USED THIS SESSION _____ GROUP I USED IT WITH _____

NOTES FOR NEXT TIME _____

_____

_____

1. When was the last time you got in trouble or goofed up because you weren't paying attention? (Examples: I missed important instructions on an assignment; got yelled at for daydreaming in class, etc.) **What are some really bad consequences that could come from not paying attention?** (An inattentive driver could have a serious accident. A student could fail college entrance tests by not paying attention.)

2. Why do you suppose anyone would fail to pay attention to something as important as salvation (vss. 1-4)? (Kids may come up with a variety of reasons: unwillingness to face the costs, failure to believe the Gospel, etc. Explain also that the Book of Hebrews was written to the Jewish people, who had been brought up believing that nothing could supersede God's written law in their Scriptures. Saying that God's Son, Jesus, had died on their behalf was a very different idea for them, so the writer reminds them of some basic truths concerning the importance of the Gospel and the miracles that accompanied its origin.)

3. Do you ever "ignore such a great salvation" (vs. 3)? In what ways? (Most of us are guilty sometimes of neglecting the truths that we've been taught. This, too, is a form of ignoring salvation.)

4. If you were transported into heaven right now, just as you are, how do you think you would feel? (The contrast between our sinful natures and God's complete holiness would be very hard on us—if it didn't make the trip impossible to begin with. We would no doubt feel unworthy to be there as soon as we got a glimpse of His glory.)

5. Since there's such a difference between sinful people and our holy God, how could God even consider giving us so many good things on earth and inviting us into heaven with Him? (Vss. 5-9—Jesus paved the way for God's acceptance of us. Jesus was "a little lower than the angels" for a while—long enough to "taste death for everyone." Sin had previously separated us from God, but Jesus brought us back into good standing.)

6. Verses 8-18 mention Jesus' suffering three times (vss. 9, 10, 18) and His death three times (vss. 9a, 9b, 14). How do you react to knowing that the One "superior to the angels" (Hebrews 1:4) willingly suffered and died for you?

7. How might "sharing in our humanity" (vs. 14) and being "made like His brothers in every way" (vs. 17) have been part of Jesus' suffering? (All of Jesus' earthly life was a humiliation compared to what He had in heaven. Encourage kids to answer from their own experiences of sadness or tough times. Point out what the passage says: Besides accepting a lower status [vs. 9], He faced hunger, pain, all the things that go with having "flesh and blood" [vs. 14], and even temptation [vs. 18].)

8. This incredibly superior Person "is not ashamed to call [us] brothers" and sisters (vs. 11). If you've ever hesitated to let people know of your relationship to Jesus, how would you explain that to Him?

9. Which of the family privileges mentioned in verses 9-18 (free from death and the fear of death, recipients of salvation, made holy, sins atoned for, help and understanding when we're tempted) have you thought about during the past month or so? Why? Which do you want to pay more attention to in the future?

10. If you wanted to explain algebra to a group of four-year-olds, how would you have to "come down to their level"? How is this similar to what happened when God became a human being named Jesus?

(Needed: Scissors for each group member)

It's easy for us to "ignore such a great salvation" by taking it for granted and overlooking the cost to Christ. The reproducible sheet, "All in the Family," will help your group members visualize the imbalance between what we receive as members of God's family and what we contribute. (You'll note that in these passages God gets nothing from us, unless you count suffering and sin.) If possible, let the Scriptures motivate some time of praise in prayer and in song.

ALL IN THE FAMILY

You know how Great Aunt Matilda is always telling you, "You got your father's ears." (Swell. So did Dumbo the Flying Elephant.) "You walk just like your mother." (Just what a guy wants to hear.) "You're going to be smart, just like your sister." (You always wanted to be able to walk and chew gum at the same time.)

Well, here's a family inheritance worth having: the benefits you get from your "big brother," Jesus. Cut out the verses (or parts of verses—some you'll have to cut in two) that describe what you get as part of His family, and line them up under the first heading. Then, just to put things in perspective, put the verses (or parts) that describe your contribution to the family under the second heading.

WHAT I GET FROM JESUS

WHAT JESUS GOT FROM ME

He [Jesus] suffered death so that by the grace of God He might taste death for everyone (vs. 9).

Both the One who makes [people] holy and those who are made holy are of the same family (vs. 11).

Since the children have flesh and blood, He too shared in their humanity so that by His death He might destroy him who holds the power of death—that is, the devil—and free those who all their lives were held in slavery by their fear of death (vss. 14, 15).

For this reason He had to be made like His brothers in every way, in order that . . . He might make atonement for the sins of the people (vs. 17).

Because He Himself suffered when He was tempted, He is able to help those who are being tempted (vs. 18).

Hard Hearts And Hot Sand

Jesus is greater even than the revered leader Moses. We must not harden our hearts against Him as the Israelites did against Moses.

(Needed: Watch with a second hand)

Distribute pens and scrap paper. Ask kids to write the names of at least five famous people (either living or dead), each on a separate piece of paper. Have them fold the pieces, and put these all in one pile. Divide into teams of three to six. Each player will have 45 seconds to get his or her team to guess as many of the names as they can. The clue-giver can say anything that does not include part of the person's name. (For example, "First U.S. President" is an acceptable clue for "George Washington.") Then explain that this chapter compares Jesus to one of the most famous people in Jewish history.

DATE I USED THIS SESSION _____ GROUP I USED IT WITH _____

NOTES FOR NEXT TIME _____

_____

_____

1. Who was your hero when you were a preschooler? When you were in fifth grade? As you've gotten older, what's changed about the things you look for in a hero?

2. To the Jewish people, Moses was a great hero. But the writer of Hebrews is stressing the one-of-a-kind qualifications of Jesus. How did the two compare? (Vss. 1-6—They played similar roles in history, leading people out of slavery—whether to Egypt or to sin—into freedom. But there could be no real comparison as to greatness. Moses was a regular human being [whom the author compares to a building]. Jesus, on the other hand, is divine [the builder]. Moses was a servant; Jesus, the Son.)

3. Why do you think Moses was such a hero for the Jewish people? After all, hadn't they whined all the way through the wilderness as he tried to lead them away from the slavery of Egypt (vss. 7-11)? (Yes, but he got the job done in spite of the people's selfish and rebellious attitudes. Similarly, Jesus makes possible the salvation of anyone who will believe, but not everyone will take Him up on His offer.)

4. It's as if the people were being given a fresh opportunity to follow a leader who could take them away from everything that enslaved them. What are some of the things that keep you from being truly free? Why is it so hard to walk away from them? Are you willing to risk letting Jesus take you beyond these things that make you feel so safe and secure? Do you ever want to turn around and go back? (Discuss some of the "enslaving" things or people in the lives of your group members, and the potential joys of a new promised land for those willing to trust Jesus completely.)

5. When is the best time to follow Jesus? ("As long as it is called Today" [vss. 12-15].) What have you done for Jesus today that you didn't do yesterday, the day before, or at any time previously? (See if kids are trying to make progress in their spiritual development, or have stopped short of where they should be.)

6. The writer of Hebrews advises believers to "Hold firmly till the end the confidence we had at first" (vs. 14). What are you less confident of today than you were when you first received Christ? What are you more confident of? How could this group help you stay confident in the Lord?

7. When the Israelites left Egypt, they resisted everything Moses (and God) were doing for them—crossing the Red Sea, being provided with daily manna, finding water . . . everything! They got all the way to the entrance of the Promised Land, thanks to Moses, but they were still complaining. Finally, God would have no more of it and barred the entrance of the land for 40 years until another, more trusting generation of people were ready (vss. 16-19). **What did this have to do with the Jewish people in Jesus' day . . . and for people today?** (God is patient and puts up with a lot of our questioning and complaining. But unless we respond to Him in faith, we will not enter the place He has prepared for us.)

8. How do you feel when you get to the end of this chapter: (a) warned, (b) nervous, (c) wanting to see what comes next, or (d) something else? How do you think the original readers felt?

The reproducible sheet, "Stuck in the Sand?" will help group members respond to this chapter's warnings. Give kids a few minutes to work on their maps. Then let them display the results. Discuss with questions like these:

• What best describes your attitude toward following God: (1) Reluctant to begin the journey; (2) on my way, but looking back; (3) trying to follow, but feeling lost much of the time; (4) just a tourist, ready to turn back if I get too bored; or (5) following my Leader and mostly enjoying the journey?

• What are some obstacles that trip you up on your journey with God?

STUCK IN THE SAND

X marks the spot. Where are you in the trek from the Land of Slavery to the Promised Land? Have you gotten started? Are you bogged down? Is the journey going well? Mark your position on this map—and feel free to draw in your own landmarks along the way.

Land of Slavery (to Sin)

Burning Sands: I'm trying, but it's getting pretty hot

Quicksand: I'm stuck in a sin that keeps pulling me down

I've given up

Mirage: I look like I'm doing better than I really am

I've been heading the wrong way

Oasis: I'm not there yet, but God is really keeping me strong

Promised Land

HEBREWS 4

Seventh-Day Stretch

We can look forward to experiencing God's rest at the end of our work if we're obedient. The sword-sharp Word of God and Jesus, the Great High Priest, point the way.

(Needed: Scissors to cut out awards)

Hand out copies of the reproducible sheet, "Well Done!" and let kids fill out awards for each member of the group. (Be sure no one is left out. If your group is large, form small groups and make sure each person fills out an award to every member of his or her small group.) Then hold an awards ceremony to present the awards. Explain that this chapter talks about the ultimate reward for people who keep serving God and who don't give up.

DATE I USED THIS SESSION _____ GROUP I USED IT WITH _____

NOTES FOR NEXT TIME _____

_____

_____

1. What's the last big project or assignment you worked on that seemed to take forever? How did you feel when you finished it?

2. God has promised that we can enter "His rest" (vs. 1). What do you think He means? How can we get in on it? (This will be an eternal reward for a job well done. We enter His rest through faith in Him—and hopefully after a lifetime of faithful Christian service.)

3. God worked six days in creating the world, and then He rested. But the Israelites, who were supposed to enter the promised land after being set free from Egypt, didn't get their rest. Why not? (Vss. 1-5—The Israelites lacked the faith to enter the rest that God wanted to give them. As a result, God made them wander in the wilderness another forty years until a more faithful generation grew up.) **Do you think this was fair? Why or why not?**

4. How could you spend forty years in church and still miss your "rest"? (Our parents can drag us to church. Our leaders can do everything possible to prepare us. But each person must respond in faith to enter.)

5. The promised land was not God's ultimate "rest area." If it were, then we're late by several thousand years. But God provided another time for us to enter His rest (vss. 6-10). Is it "Today" (vs. 7) or in the future? (The ultimate "rest" lies ahead while the work goes on, but the decision to enter God's rest must be made now. And those who receive Christ can experience a preview of that rest now: "rest" from being a slave to sin and worry.)

6. What kind of "rest" do the following kids really need: (a) a senior who worries constantly about not being able to get into college; (b) a seventh grader who's always trying to be funny in order to get others to like him; (c) a ninth grade girl who's stealing to support a drug habit? (Through obedience, we can experience God's peace and contentment even before we get to our place of ultimate rest. This may mean [a] trusting God for our futures, [b] trusting Him for friends and letting God change us to be more like His

Son, or [c] turning our backs on sin and becoming part of a supportive group of Christians.)

7. **Why do you think the writer of Hebrews suddenly switches from "rest" to talking about the Bible (vss. 12, 13)?** (Verse 11 warns us not to miss our eternal rest by disobeying God. Scripture keeps us on track by showing us whether our thoughts and attitudes are right.)

8. **The Word of God here** (vss. 12, 13) **sounds almost dangerous. Is that how you see the Bible? Have you ever felt "uncovered" when you read the Bible? When?**

9. **According to verses 14 through 16, Jesus acts as our "high priest," interceding for us (as a lawyer might) before God. When was the last time you needed a good heavenly lawyer? Could you have "pleaded your own case" before God?**

10. **Since He experienced every temptation we do, Jesus knows exactly how we feel. If you could ask Him how He dealt with a particular temptation, what would it be?** (Let kids just think about this if they'd rather not reply aloud.)

11. **When you pray or think about your relationship with God, is it "with confidence"** (vs. 16)? (Point out that Jesus is not out to get us when we fall short; He "sympathize[s] with our weaknesses" [vs. 15] and wants to help.)

Brainstorm some temptations young people face today, and how Jesus might have faced the same kind of temptation in that earlier culture. (He probably wasn't tempted to cheat on an exam, but the devil tried to get Him to take a "short cut" to success [Matthew 4:5-7]. Sexual temptations, family frictions, pressures for substance abuse take different forms but remain much the same.) Kids may feel irreverent even thinking about Jesus facing sexual temptation and the like; remind them that being tempted is not the sin—giving in is. Hebrews tells us that Jesus knows just what we are facing—and He is able and willing to help us overcome it. Encourage kids to memorize verse 15 as an encouragement when they're tempted.

Well Done!

Look around you. Your mild-mannered peers are actually award-winning citizens. Pick out an appropriate award for *every* member of the group, and be ready to explain why you think he or she qualifies for it.

For friendliness to everyone, I hereby present

name _____

with the SUPERNOVA SMILE award.

For good suggestions and ideas, I hereby present

name _____

with the EDISON LIGHT BULB award.

For keeping discussions going, I hereby present

name _____

with the SPEAK YOUR MIND award.

WINNER

For a good sense of humor, I hereby present

name _____

with the COMEDY CLUB award.

WINNER

For helping everyone get along, I hereby present

name _____

with the DOVE OF PEACE

WINNER

For faithful attendance, I hereby present

name _____

with the COUNT ON ME award

For respecting others' opinions, I hereby present

name _____

with the LISTEN AS MUCH AS YOU TALK award.

For being positive and enthusiastic, I hereby present

name _____

with the MORALE BOOSTER award.

For making things interesting, I hereby present

name _____

with the KEEP ME AWAKE award.

HEBREWS 5

Food for Thought

Just as Old Testament high priests were appointed to stand before God on behalf of the people of Israel, Jesus acts as our high priest before His Father. As we learn more about such things, we need to grow in the faith and not remain at a "baby" stage.

(Needed: Team prize [optional])

Divide your group into teams, lined up in relay style at one end of the room. You stand at the other end. Have each team appoint a captain. Explain that you will ask for a series of items (one at a time) that must be carried to you by the team captain only. The first captain to provide you with the item will be awarded a point. Suggested items include a shoelace, a pen, an earring, a single hair (not from the team captain), a group member (who must be carried), 17¢, a sock, etc. As you continue with the session, explain that the role of the high priest was to do on a spiritual level what your team captains did for the others physically—receive an "offering" and give it to the one requesting it.

DATE I USED THIS SESSION _____ GROUP I USED IT WITH _____

NOTES FOR NEXT TIME _____

_____

_____

1. What do you think of when I say the word "priest"? How about "high priest"?

2. Under the Old Testament system you would take the priest your offerings, he would go offer them to God, and you would be forgiven for your sins for a short time. Then later you'd come back and do it all again. What do you think you'd like about that system? What wouldn't you like? (Some may like the predictability; some may think it would be easier to make sacrifices every few months than to be a continual "living sacrifice." Others may not like the idea of killing animals for sacrifice, or the formality and inconvenience of the rituals.)

3. When you've done something wrong, how do you get forgiveness from God? (Probably through prayer.) Have you ever felt like you needed to make some kind of "sacrifice," too? (Sometimes people try to overcome guilt feelings by hoping to "balance things out" with a good deed. We need to turn from doing wrong and ask God's forgiveness, but forgiveness comes only through Christ's sacrificial death.)

4. How would you have liked being an Old Testament priest when it came to reminding people that they needed to have their sins forgiven (vss. 1-3)? (It required that the person "deal gently" with others, since the priest had sins of his own. In fact, before the priest could offer sacrifices on behalf of the other people, he had to perform a separate sacrifice for himself and his family.)

5. The position of "priest" wasn't an elected one; it was restricted to the tribe of Levi—designated by God. Jesus, however, was from the tribe of Judah. Why didn't this cause a problem? (Vss. 4-6—Jesus, too, was chosen by God. Rather than being a priest in the tradition of the Levites, Jesus was a priest "in the order of Melchizedek," who predated Levi. [See Hebrews 7 and Genesis 14:18-20.])

6. What does Jesus' priesthood (vss. 7-10) mean to you personally? (Jesus is not only a *priest* of God; He is also the *Son* of God. It should be a comforting thought to know that the one who represents us before God is the very one who died for our sins.)

7. As the writer of Hebrews is explaining all these things to his readers, he suddenly stops and begins to address them directly. Suppose you were in the group having this message read to you, and suddenly you heard verses 11-14. How would you feel? What do you think you would do?

8. Which of the following charges would you have to plead "guilty" to: (a) "You are slow to learn"; (b) "By this time you ought to be teachers"; (c) "You need someone to teach you the elementary truths of God's Word all over again" (d) "You need milk, not solid food"? What could you say in your defense? If the "court" appointed a counselor to help you with these problems, what would you want him or her to do?

9. What are some "spiritual" activities that could be put in the "milk" category? (Church attendance without real involvement; coming to youth group for the volleyball rather than the Bible studies; prayers for petty or selfish concerns, etc.)

10. How have you tried "solid food"? (Examples: Early morning devotions instead of extra sleep; speaking up for Jesus in groups; prayers for others, etc.) **How did these things work out?**

11. On a scale of 1 (milk) to 10 (T-bone steak), where's your level of spiritual development right now?

Continue your examination of the milk/meat contrast with the reproducible sheet, "Supermarket Shelf." After group members complete their sheets, discuss: **What are the first steps you need to take in moving from milk to meat? How can this group help you in your personal growth? Do we try to do too much for you, so that you don't develop on your own? What opportunities do you need in order to move to a higher level of maturity?**

SUPERMARKETSHELF

Check out **Hebrews 5:11-14.** Then *register* **how your spiritual "diet" is doing by circling your usual choices in this supermarket. Are you bottle-fed, eating baby food, chomping junk food, or eating the real grownup stuff?**

AISLE 1

Bible knowledge and reading

BIBLE BOTTLE
Scripture-flavored formula for babies

STRAINED SCRIPTURE PORTIONS
Tiny bites of sweetened verses for the immature palate

SCRIPTURE CHIPS
Bits of Bible, but mostly deep-fried, nacho-flavored filler

MEATY MEALS
Juicy chunks of God's Word that you can chew yourself

AISLE 2

Prayer

NO-PRAY FORMULA
Why pray when adults can do it for you?

SINGSONG PRAYER CRACKERS
Nothing tougher than "Now I lay me down to sleep"

PRAYER POPS
Candy flavored with lots of meaningless but spiritual-sounding phrases

AMEN PRAYER DINNERS
Real communication for real people

AISLE 3

Worship

SLEEPYTIME JUICE
Rock-a-bye your way through the church service

CAP'N CHURCH CEREAL
Sugary morsels to keep you entertained

CHURCH CHEWING GUM
Keep your jaw moving but your brain turned off

CELEBRATION BANQUET
Get in there and tell God how you feel about His love!

HEBREWS 6

Grow Up!

Christians should keep maturing spiritually as they give up old habits and move toward godliness. God has promised to bless those who genuinely seek Him.

Ask group members to provide the kinds of words (noun, adjective, etc.) needed on the reproducible sheet, "This Isn't Your Life." Fill in the blanks without letting them see the story. After all the blanks are filled, read the story aloud to the group. Then explain that Hebrews 6 talks a lot about the direction our lives should take as we grow up.

DATE I USED THIS SESSION _____ GROUP I USED IT WITH _____

NOTES FOR NEXT TIME _____

_____

_____

1. If you could travel back in time and tell yourself something when you were a first grader, what would it be? What would you tell the fifth-grade you?

2. How has your faith in God changed since you were four years old? Seven years old? How has it changed since last year? (See whether answers reflect a growing relationship. Childlike faith is good, but at some point we also need to think about doctrine and deeper questions about God.)

3. As you look around our church, who are some people you think of as spiritually grown-up? What are some things that keep you from being more like them? (Examples: Lack of effort; lack of time; waiting until I get old; don't want to be like them, etc.)

4. What are some things about being age 21 that make you want to be that old? (Freedom, earning money, etc.) What are some things about being a more mature Christian that could be better than being an immature one? (Knowing God better, feeling you can trust Him; being able to answer more questions from non-Christians; being better able to resist some temptations, etc.)

5. If you wanted to "go on to maturity" (vss. 1-3) and learn things about Scripture you don't know, how could you start? (Personal Bible study; group study of a book of the Bible; study commentaries or books about the Bible, etc.)

6. Scholars disagree over what verses 4-6 mean. Many don't believe that Christians who make a genuine commitment to God can lose their salvation. How would you interpret these verses? (Discuss your church's position if possible. Some believe the passage teaches that Christians can lose their salvation. Some think the writer's argument is hypothetical, to make the point that we should get serious about spiritual maturity. Some say it doesn't refer to genuine Christians, but to people who got close enough to see what it was all about and claimed to be Christians, yet never completely yielded to God.)

7. When land responds to rain, you can tell a difference (vss. 7, 8). **If 50% of the kids at your school responded to Jesus by receiving Him, what kinds of differences would you expect?** (Encourage specific examples.)

8. **How do you think the Hebrew Christians felt when they heard verses 9-12? How do you feel when you apply those verses to yourself?**

9. Some people say, "I swear to God" (which they shouldn't do). **When God wants to assure us of something, what does He do?** (Vss. 13-18—He has sworn by Himself, since no other power is greater. The fact that He said it was enough for Him. But He affirmed it with an oath for the sake of people accustomed to hearing one.)

10. **How is your hope in God's promises most like an anchor in your life** (vss. 19, 20): **(a) Keeps me steady when I face doubts; (b) keeps me from drifting into sin; (c) keeps me from having fun by weighing me down; (d) keeps me from changing?**

11. **Who is Melchizedek** (vs. 20)? **After reading Genesis 14:17-21, how much do you know about him?** (Not too much. It seems he did know Abraham's God, which was rare during that time. He blessed Abraham, who gave him a tenth of the spoils from a victory [which was a king's share]. More will be said about him in chapter 7.)

Use the imagery of verses 7 and 8 to help group members assess their receptiveness to the Word of God (the "rain") and their fruitfulness (the "crop" or "thorns"). Distribute paper and pens and instruct each to draw a landscape (anything from desert to rain forest) that represents his or her spiritual life right now. Have kids show their finished works. Say: **If anything is growing at all in your landscape, there's something for God to work with. If not, the next step is to get some seeds planted and watered.** Encourage kids to be specific about what they'd like to see happen next in their landscapes. If several students need to take similar steps, perhaps they can work together in small groups.

THiS ISN'T YOUR LIFE

*W*hen _____ *(group member)* was born, his/her mother thought he/she was the

most _____ *(adjective)* baby on _____ *(planet)*. Weighing in at

_____ *(number)* pounds, _____ *(number)* ounces, he/she was the most

_____ *(geometrical shape)* baby in the church nursery—although

_____ *(another group member)* came close. _____ 's *(first group*

member) best friends growing up were _____ and _____ *(group*

members). The three of them loved to play _____ *(sport)* and talk about

_____ *(plural noun)*. _____ *(first group member)* excelled in

_____ *(school subject)*, although he/she was not as good in _____

(school subject). He/she eventually went to school for _____ *(number)* years, training

for _____ *(career)*. He/she seriously dated _____ *(famous person of*

the opposite sex) for a long time, but ended up marrying _____ *(another famous*

person of the opposite sex). The happy couple moved to _____ *(place)* and had

_____ *(number)* children. _____ *(first group member)* will always be

remembered for his/her famous expression, "_____" *(exclamation)*.

HEBREWS 7

Replacing Those Levi's

The writer of Hebrews explains carefully how Jesus acts as high priest on our behalf—not as a Levite, which the Jewish people were accustomed to, but as Melchizedek, who served as priest even before the Levites existed.

(Needed: Parts of two puzzles)

Give kids a jigsaw puzzle to assemble within a time limit. But replace one piece with a piece from a different puzzle (without telling the kids). (Note: If you want to make this a contest, form teams and use two puzzles.) When kids end up with an incomplete puzzle and a piece that doesn't fit, explain: **This is how many of the Hebrews felt when they heard about Jesus as a priest. It just didn't fit the picture. This chapter tries to explain how Jesus really is the missing piece in the priesthood as they knew it.**

DATE I USED THIS SESSION _____ GROUP I USED IT WITH _____

NOTES FOR NEXT TIME _____

_____

_____

1. Describe someone who's completely shattered your idea of a traditional role. For example, have you ever known a "house husband" who loved staying home with the kids while his wife worked? A female football player who could really hold her own "with the guys"?

2. The writer of this chapter is going to shatter some ideas about the traditional priest's role, too. From what you know of Jesus, can you think of any traditional ideas he turned upside down during His time on earth? (He died on a cross instead of leading an armed rebellion as some hoped the Messiah would; He came back from the dead; He kept angering the religious leaders by contradicting them and calling them hypocrites, etc.)

3. The beginning of this chapter summarizes what Genesis 14:17-21 says about Melchizedek, then adds some comments (vss. 1-3). **What do you think the writer is getting at?** (Note the similarities between Melchizedek and Jesus. The writer is setting up a comparison to demonstrate that Jesus, like Melchizedek, is of a higher order of priests.)

4. What's the point of all the talk about who paid whom a tenth (vss. 4-10)? (The writer continues to makes the point that priest Melchizedek was greater than even the respected priests from the tribe of Levi; you might even say the Levite priests paid their tenth to Melchizedek.)

5. In verses 11-18 the writer really gets to the point: Jesus is a priest "in the order of Melchizedek, not in the order of Aaron [a Levite]" (vs. 11). **What were some of the differences between those two kinds of priesthoods?**

To help answer this question, work through the reproducible sheet, "Order! Order!" at this point in the discussion. The comparison should help group members keep all these details straight.

6. One thing that didn't change was the *job* of high priest: to stand before God and represent a sinful group of people, asking for mercy and forgiveness. How is Jesus the best priest for this? (Vss. 23-28—He's a permanent priest [always there]; He can save completely; He needs no sacrifice for Himself; the sacrifice He offers on our behalf is not some animal, but rather His own blood; His sacrifice doesn't need to be repeated but is "once for all;" He is not weak, but perfect.)

7. When you hear that you're sinful enough that Jesus had to die for you, how do you feel? Offended? Guilty? Grateful? Something else? How would most kids at school react to the idea that they're sinners, too?

8. If we can approach God directly in prayer with our confessions, praise, and requests, why do we need a high priest? Is this chapter just for the Hebrews of the first century? How does it apply to us? (The early Hebrew Christians needed to be reminded that Jesus is the great high priest so that they would *dare* approach God's throne with confidence [4:16], praying in the name of Jesus. Going to God without a human intermediary was new and foreign to them. We may need to be reminded not to take that privilege for granted; it's possible only because Jesus precedes us as high priest. We often use other words [mediator, intercessor, etc.], but the meaning is the same.)

9. Have you ever "approached" God on someone else's behalf by praying for that person? What happened? Have you ever agreed to pray for someone, only to forget? How does this compare with Christ's work in heaven for us? (Christ never forgets to be our mediator.)

10. If you had to get this chapter's point across in a rap video, what would be the first four lines of the script? What kinds of pictures would you want to show?

To make all this practical, discuss specific reasons group members need their High Priest, Jesus, to represent them before God today. (Examples: Confession of specific sins; prayer requests; intercession for other friends or family members, etc.) Talk a little about how Jesus' unique qualities (that kids listed on the reproducible sheet and discussed in question 5) can give us confidence as we bring our needs to Him. Then spend some time in prayer, being sure to include adoration for those qualities that set Jesus above all other high priests.

ORDER! ORDER!

The writer of this letter to the Hebrews made a big point of comparing the Old Testament priests ("in the order of Levi") with Jesus ("in the order of Melchizedek.") Most of us probably don't know as much as those early Hebrew Christians did about priests in *any* order, so let's spend a little time figuring out the differences. Fill in the spaces and see how these two orders stack up.

	The Order of Levi	The Order of Melchizedek
From the tribe of . . .	(vs. 5) _____	(vs. 14) _____
On the basis of . . .	(vs. 16) _____	(vs. 16) _____
Lasting value:	(vs. 18) _____	(vs. 19) _____
Length of service:	(vs. 23) _____	(vs. 24) _____
Must sacrifice for the sins of . . .	(vs. 27) _____	(vs. 26) _____
Frequency of sacrifices needed:	(vs. 27) _____	(vs. 27) _____
Appointed by . . .	(vs. 28) _____	(vs. 28) _____
Quality:	(vs. 28) _____	(vs. 28) _____

HEBREWS 8

It's New!
It's for You!

The agreement God had with the Old Testament Israelites is replaced by a new and lasting covenant, of which the previous one was a foreshadowing.

(Needed: Team prize [optional])

Divide into teams and have them compete to come up with the oldest and newest of each item you call for. (Some sample items: penny, haircut, braces, piece of jewelry, team member.) After the contest, explain that this chapter contrasts old and new covenants—agreements between God and His people.

DATE I USED THIS SESSION _____ GROUP I USED IT WITH _____

NOTES FOR NEXT TIME _____

_____

_____

1. Suppose you have just been arrested for murder, and if convicted, will receive the death penalty. What immediate steps would you take? (Call parents; call a lawyer; deny all guilt; start praying, etc.) Would you talk to people and try to find which lawyer was best, or would you just call whoever was first in the phone book?

2. You've probably heard that "the wages of sin is death" (Romans 6:23). God is a righteous judge who must sentence those who are guilty (which we all are). If you were the lawyer for the human race, would you plead guilty, innocent by reason of insanity, or something else? What witnesses could you call? What might be your "closing argument"?

3. When it came to dealing with God on behalf of sinful clients, who were the "lawyers" of the Old Testament? (It was the role of the high priest to approach God and sacrifice for the sins of the people.) Even though human priests had performed to the best of their abilities, how is Jesus an even more effective priest? (Vss. 1, 2—Human priests were limited by their personal sinfulness. Jesus has no such limitation. He also serves as priest from heaven, not in an earthly temple.)

4. Human high priests were examples of what Jesus would be (vss. 3, 4). The temple (or tabernacle) was only a "copy and shadow of what is in heaven" (vs. 5). If you had been one of the Hebrews, how do you think you would have responded to these statements? (Examples: With fear, wanting to keep what I've known all my life; anger at such "blasphemy"; eagerness to know more.)

5. God had a covenant—a legal, binding agreement—with the Old Testament Israelites. But now He has made a new one with us (vss. 6, 7). Does that mean He changed His mind, or that He likes us better than He did the Old Testament believers? Explain. (No. God honors every covenant and promise He makes. But things went wrong with the first covenant [vs. 7]—not because of God's fault but because of the people's fault [vs. 8].)

6. The difference between a promise and a covenant is that a promise is based on the intentions of a single person. A covenant is an agreement between two or more people. How did the Israelites let down their side of the deal? (Vss. 8, 9—Even though God delivered them safely out of the slavery of Egypt, they complained a lot and turned to idols when they were on their own.)

7. If you'd signed a contract to buy a new motorcycle, but the dealer tried to substitute a used one at the last minute, would you be willing to give the dealer a second chance? If you and a friend agreed to meet at the mall every Saturday at noon, but the friend stood you up for three Saturdays in a row, would you be willing to try again? How are the actions of the dealer and the friend like those of the Israelites?

8. God was willing to make a new and better agreement with His people, making it easier for them to have a living, working relationship with Him (vss. 10-12), what does that tell you about God? (That He actually wants to relate to human beings; that He's forgiving; that He's willing to give us a new start.) How has God given you a "second chance"?

9. When we discover God's new and better way to live, what should happen to our old way of relating to Him and to others? (Vs. 13—The things that don't work [such as our attempted salvation by works, being too afraid of God to think of Him as Father, or whatever] first become old and eventually become "obsolete.") Is there anything from your "old life" that you're still hanging on to?

Because this chapter focuses on what God has done for His people, at first glance it may not seem to call for much personal application. But remind your group members that the new covenant, like every contract, has *two* parts—God's and ours. The Israelites of the Old Testament reneged on their end of the old contract. How are your group members doing in response to the new one? The reproducible sheet, "Covenant Contract," will help them evaluate their obedience and recommit to being partners with God.

COVENANT
C O N T R A C T

A covenant, like a contract, is an agreement between two or more people. As God calls people to Him and offers forgiveness of sins and eternal life, He makes some promises. A few, taken from Hebrews 8, are:

• I will put My laws in their minds and write them on their hearts (Benefit to you: Knowing what God wants of you and knowing His guidelines for living)

• I will be their God, and they will be My people (Benefit to you: God's love, loyalty, and protection)

• They will all know Me (Benefit to you: A personal relationship with God)

• I will forgive their wickedness and will remember their sins no more (Benefit to you: Salvation and forgiveness)

Now it's your turn. How are you doing at keeping up your end of the deal? Check all the boxes that apply.

☐ I pay so much attention to God's will and laws that they're engraved on my heart (I'm willing to follow them) and mind (I've made them part of my thinking)

☐ I honor and worship God as *my* God, and I live so that others can tell I'm one of His people

☐ I make knowing Him a priority—through reading His Word and through communication in prayer and worship

☐ I ask for forgiveness for my sins and try to make disobeying Him a thing of the past

God never breaks His side of the deal. But maybe you need to recommit to your part. If you're not serious, leave the bottom of this page blank. Covenants are serious contracts, not New Year's resolutions. But if you're willing to do one or more things to try to become more obedient to God and get closer to Him, list those things below.

In the weeks to come, I covenant (promise), with the help of the Holy Spirit, to try to respond to God's covenant by:

Signed _____ Date _____

For Better or For Worship

Worship in the Old Testament tabernacle was based on external regulations and could not clean the conscience, but Christ's blood makes us inwardly clean so that we can truly serve the living God.

Have the group act out the skit on the reproducible sheet, "The Church of the Golden Chipmunk." After having a good time with it, discuss: **Why was Chris so uncomfortable? What words and symbols that we use in church might be confusing to "outsiders"? Which do you find confusing sometimes? What parts of the church service help you worship? Which don't?** Explain that Hebrews 9 is also about worship—and some of the symbols and actions that were part of Old Testament ceremonies.

DATE I USED THIS SESSION _____ GROUP I USED IT WITH _____

NOTES FOR NEXT TIME _____

_____

_____

1. **What symbols of God or the Christian faith can you find in this room?** (If time allows, let kids roam the church to see who can come up with the longest list of Christian symbols—stained glass windows, crosses, communion table, maps showing missions work, pictures in the primary classroom, etc.) **How do these symbols remind us of God? Can they also limit our ideas of Him?** (God is a Spirit. Any time we try to represent Him in words or art, we fall short.)

2. **Have you ever bought something you had to assemble yourself before you could use it, and it just about drove you crazy to put it together? What happened?** (After kids respond, explain that Old Testament worship was sometimes much the same way. People who wanted to be closer to God first had to deal with animal sacrifices, the priests, eating the right foods, and numerous other rules.)

3. **One of the first rules for worship involved the place— the tabernacle (vss. 1-5). God's presence was signified in the most holy place in the center of the tabernacle, which could be entered only once a year, and then only by the high priest (vss. 6, 7). How would you like it if you could worship God in only one place?** (Perhaps some of your kids do confine their worship activities to church. If so, don't downgrade having a special place for worship, but point out the need to worship God at all times and places.)

4. **Much of the worship at the tabernacle involved outward actions that really didn't help the worshiper have a clean conscience (vss. 8-10). Can you think of any parts of our worship that sometimes become just outward actions for you?** (Examples: Prayers that we tune out; sermons we don't listen to; anything we do on "autopilot" instead of from the heart.)

5. **How can a personal relationship with Jesus make worship internal, not just external?** (Vss. 11-15—Jesus has taken care of all the external requirements so that we can have the internal benefits: clean consciences, the Holy Spirit, true service to the living God.)

6. **Do you know if you're named in anyone's will? Maybe your parents'? Are you eager to get your inheritance?**

(Kids might like to get the money, but probably don't wish the person were dead. Compare answers to verses 15-18. For us to receive an inheritance from Jesus, He had to die.)

7. How do you think you would have liked the Old Testament method of cleansing (vss. 19-22)? If "without the shedding of blood there is no forgiveness" [vs. 22], why don't we have blood in our worship now? (Christ's blood is the ultimate sacrifice for the forgiveness of sins [vss. 23-28]; we don't need any more. But remind group members that we *do* still remember blood in our worship—in a very different way—every time we celebrate the Lord's Supper.)

8. Do you think worship was harder in Old Testament times, or now? (In some ways our worship may be "easier" because Christ has taken care of all the requirements [vss. 24-28]. But we are to offer *ourselves* as living sacrifices [Romans 12:1], not just some animal once a year. And true worship requires us to involve all of ourselves, including our thoughts and feelings.)

9. Someday all believers will worship God together in heaven. Are you hoping to (a) get lots of practice now, (b) avoid heaven completely, (c) be changed when you go to heaven so that you like worship more than you do now, or (d) something else?

Say: **Long ago, in a tabernacle far, far away, people worshiped God. They had numerous cumbersome rules to follow before their offerings could be accepted. But then, about 2,000 years ago, Jesus died and rose from the dead. So you no longer need to go to a tabernacle and offer sacrifices. You can worship God anytime. Anywhere. By yourself or in a crowd. Loudly or quietly. Laughing or crying. But do you? Now that you have the freedom to worship as you please, do you take advantage of it? Or do you still just show up at church and do what they tell you to do?** Brainstorm two lists of group members' worship habits—one "External," like "Bowing for prayer, but not listening," and one "Internal," like "Seeing a beautiful sunset and thanking God on the spot." Try to come up with as many internal, spontaneous kinds of worship as you can.

The Church of the Golden Chipmunk

Cast: Chris, Jo, Leader, and Congregation (played by the rest of the group)

CHRIS *(entering the room)*: So, this is your church, huh? You've been inviting me to come here for so long, I figured I'd better check it out.

JO *(leading CHRIS to a seat and sitting down in the next seat)*: I know you'll like it. It'll change your life.

LEADER *(to all)*: Welcome, friends, to the Church of the Golden Chipmunk. I'm your Head Acorn, Number Eleven Smith. Before we bow our elbows for the Altercation, let us Samsonize.

CHRIS *(whispering to JO)*: What? What did he say?

JO: Shhhhh. You're supposed to Samsonize. Take that BarkBook and turn to number ChiChi.

CHRIS: What?

CONGREGATION *(singing to the tune of "Twinkle, Twinkle Little Star")*: Golden Chipmunk, we love you, climbing oaks and twirling true. Help us crack the acorn shell, something that you do so well. Golden Chipmunk, we love you, climbing oaks and twirling true.

CHRIS: Was that a hymn, or what?

JO: Shhhhh. It's time for announcements.

LEADER: I see we have a visitor with us this morning. Little Acorn Jo, would you like to introduce your guest?

JO *(standing)*: This is my friend Chris.

LEADER: Let's all give Chris a Golden Chipmunk welcome!

CONGREGATION: Chichichichi—Chipmunk! *(They applaud.)*

LEADER: Jo, perhaps your friend would like to wear the Frisky Hello Hat.

CHRIS: Uh, no, I don't think so.

CONGREGATION: Boooooooo!

LEADER: Maybe your friend would rather pin the Fuzzy Tail of Faith to his left ear and kneel before the Shining Bulooka of Nernablab.

CHRIS: Huh? Uh, no!

CONGREGATION: Boooooooo!

JO: Oh, come on, Chris! Then you can tell us how the Treetops have been especially meaningful to you this week!

CHRIS: I'm outta here! You guys are all—nuts! *(CHRIS exits.)*

LEADER: Well—of course we are! Right, Little Acorns?

CONGREGATION: Yaaaaaay! *(They applaud.)*

HEBREWS 10

Out of the Shadows

The Old Testament sacrifices provided pictures of Christ's perfect sacrifice. Since Jesus has opened the way to God, we should reject sin and confidently keep living for Him.

(Needed: A slide projector or bright light, variety of objects)

Set up a slide projector or bright light that will shine on a wall of your meeting place. One at a time, hold up a number of objects (a quarter, paper clip, watch, spoon, etc.) and see if kids can identify them by the shadows cast. Then, while the light is set up, let the kids cut loose with their best shadow animals. Finally, explain that the Old Testament system of sacrifices was a "shadow" of what Jesus was going to do.

DATE I USED THIS SESSION _____ GROUP I USED IT WITH _____

NOTES FOR NEXT TIME _____

_____

_____

1. Have you ever seen an animal killed? How did it make you feel?

2. The Old Testament system of animal sacrifice seems cruel to many people today. Why do you think God required it? (The death of the animal was a reminder of the sin of the person offering it [vss. 1-4]. While it may have been unpleasant to witness the slaughter, it was a graphic preview of what sinful people were going to do to God's own perfect Son [vss. 5-10].)

3. Verse 13 says that Christ is waiting for "his enemies to be made his footstool." Which of the following comes closest to your reaction to that: (a) "What is He waiting for? Let's get on with it"; (b) "I'm glad He's waiting, because . . . "? Explain.

4. On a scale of 0 to 100 percent, how much do you think you've experienced these benefits described in verses 11-18?
  • Being made perfect and holy;
  • Having God's laws written on your heart and mind;
  • Really feeling that God has forgiven and forgotten your sins.
On the same scale, how much do you *want* those three benefits?

5. Verses 19-23 advise us to have confidence in approaching God, sincerity, assurance, a clean conscience, and hope. Which of these qualities can be faked? Which can't? Why might somebody try to fake them? (We might try to fake these to impress other Christians, but we and God wouldn't be fooled.)

6. How have people tried to "spur [you] on toward love and good deeds" [vs. 25]? How did you respond? (Discuss the difference between nagging and motivating.)

7. What are some of the things people miss out on if they're "in the habit" of not meeting together [vs. 24]? (Encouragement, fellowship, the "spurring on" talked about in verse 24, worship, spiritual growth, etc.)

8. Why would anyone deliberately keep sinning after hearing the good news about Christ? (They might think, "I'll deal with that later"; they might prefer the short-term "fun" of sin to an eternal reward they can't see, etc.) **Do you think people hear the "bad news" of verses 26-31 often enough? Why or why not?**

9. How do you feel when you read verses 26-31? Do you feel scared for yourself or for anyone you know? What can you do about that?

10. How might people today "trample the Son of God underfoot," treat Christ's blood as unholy, or "insult the Spirit of grace"? (Some commentators feel this passage refers specifically to those who commit the sin of apostasy; in a sense, though, any deliberate sin is like doing one of these terrible things [vs. 26].)

11. Have you had to deal with any of the problems described in verses 32-34? Do you think the promises in verses 35-39 would be enough to keep you going if you did have to face that kind of trouble?

12. When was the last time you found yourself "shrinking back" (vs. 39) from doing what you knew was right? If you could live that time over again, what would you do differently?

(Needed: Die, game pieces)

The reproducible sheet, "Let's Go!" is a response to the commands in verses 22-25. Divide into teams of four or fewer. Have teams take turns rolling a die, moving their game piece (coins or other small objects are fine for game pieces), and giving an example of how to apply the command on the square they've landed on. Designate a recorder to write down each response under the appropriate category to make sure no team repeats what another has said. When the game is over, ask: **Which of these four things is hardest for you to do? Which is easiest? What can the group do to help you in these areas?**

Let's GO!

When people want to inspire someone to action, they often say, "Let's. . . ." Think about it. "Let's go to the mall." "Let's play softball." "Let's go take another look at that new checkout person at King McBurger."

When the writer of Hebrews wanted his readers to act, he used a similar term—four times, as a matter of fact. For each of his four calls to action, see how many specific ways you can think of to do what he says.

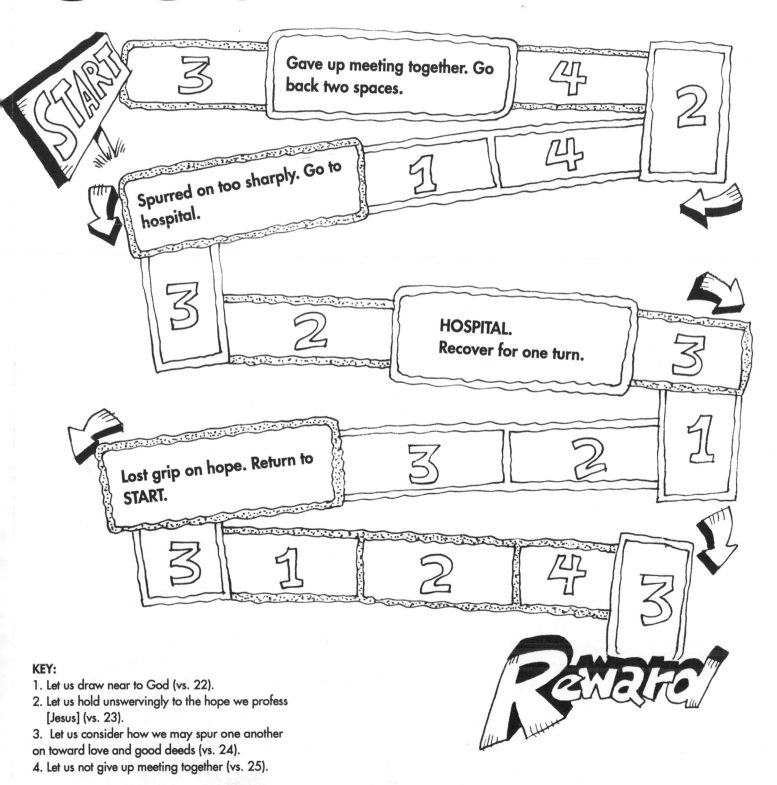

START

3 | Gave up meeting together. Go back two spaces. | **4** | **2**

Spurred on too sharply. Go to hospital. | **1** | **4**

3 | **2** | HOSPITAL. Recover for one turn. | **3**

1

Lost grip on hope. Return to START. | **3** | **2**

3 | **1** | **2** | **4** | **3**

Reward!

KEY:
1. Let us draw near to God (vs. 22).
2. Let us hold unswervingly to the hope we profess [Jesus] (vs. 23).
3. Let us consider how we may spur one another on toward love and good deeds (vs. 24).
4. Let us not give up meeting together (vs. 25).

HEBREWS 11

Faith Hall of Fame

CHAPTER ✓ CHECK

Faith is explained by definition and example. The examples come from a sort of Old Testament hall of fame—people including Abraham, Noah, Rahab, Moses, and Joseph.

OPENING ACT

(Needed: Team prize [optional])

Before the session, copy and cut up the reproducible sheet, "The Hall of Fame Game." You'll need one copy per team. When the session starts, form teams and explain the game. You'll be giving each team a slip of paper that contains a category and five letters of the alphabet. Teams will have one minute to come up with names (last names only) that fit the category and that start with the five letters (one name per letter). Teams get one point for each correct name, *plus five points for each correct name that no other team mentions.* Hand out the "Sports Hall of Fame" slips and give the "Go" signal. After a minute, tally up points. (You be the judge of which names really fit the categories.) Repeat with the other slips as time allows. Award a team prize if you wish. Then explain that Hebrews 11 is a "Faith Hall of Fame." See whether kids can name any of the "Faith Hall of Famers" without looking at the chapter.

DATE I USED THIS SESSION _____ GROUP I USED IT WITH _____

NOTES FOR NEXT TIME _____

_____

_____

1. Somebody has said, "Faith is believing something you know isn't true." What's wrong with that definition?

2. Can you remember a time when you took a risk and placed a lot of faith in God? If so, could you tell us about it? (The salvation experience would certainly qualify here, but also press for post-salvation stories of times when group members were so faithful [or perhaps desperate] that they were willing to leave the outcome of a major crisis in God's hands alone. Such instances might include facing the death of a loved one, deciding to risk personal reputation and live as a Christian should, etc.)

3. Is the definition of faith (vs. 1) a contradiction, or can we really be "certain of what we do not see"? (We can be certain that the wind is blowing, that gravity is in effect, etc. We can judge by results when we don't see a physical object. But it's pretty easy to believe in wind and gravity when everyone around us does. There is evidence for the existence of God, but it takes faith to decide for certain that God is really there.)

4. It takes faith to believe that God created the universe (vs. 3). What are some other things you need faith to believe? (The virgin birth, eternal life, etc.) What about Christianity is easiest for you to believe? What is hardest?

5. What's your favorite Old Testament story? Why? (Let kids respond, and then see how many are included in the list in Hebrews 11.)

6. What do you remember most (or what can you discover) about the following people?
• **Cain and Abel** (vs. 4; Genesis 4:1-16)
• **Gideon** (vs. 32; Judges 6—8)
• **Enoch** (vss. 5, 6; Genesis 5:21-24)
• **Barak** (vs. 32; Judges 4—5)
• **Noah** (vs. 7; Genesis 6—9)
• **Samson** (vs. 32; Judges 13—16)
• **Abraham** (vss. 8-19; Genesis 12—22)
• **Jephthah** (vs. 32; Judges 11—12)
• **Joseph** (vs. 22; Genesis 37; 39—50)
• **David** (vs. 32; I Samuel 16—I Kings 2)

- **Moses** (vss. 23-29; Book of Exodus)
- **Samuel** (vs. 32; I Samuel 1—16)
- **Isaac, Jacob, and Esau** (vss. 20-21; Genesis 24—33)
- **Joshua, Rahab, and the spies** (vss. 30-31; Joshua 2—6)

(As you review some or all of these stories, check for new information provided in Hebrews 11 that isn't in the Old Testament accounts—God's pleasure with Enoch [vs. 5], Abraham's belief in God's power to resurrect the dead [vs. 19], etc.)

7. **Can you name anyone who underwent one of the experiences listed in verses 33-38?**

8. **What was extra-special about the faith of all these people?** (Vss. 39, 40—They had only been *promised* a Savior. They had much less to base their faith on than do we, who have a written record of the Savior.)

9. **What do we need to learn from the examples of all these people?** (It's not just a nice thing to have faith. Rather, faith is *essential* to please God. [See verse 6.])

10. **What do you need to trust God for most during the coming year? What do you hope for? What in this chapter can help you become more sure of what you hope for?**

Say: **You probably couldn't match Arnold Schwartzenegger's muscles if you were in the early stages of body building—or Elle McPherson's looks the first time you applied makeup. You also probably can't expect to start out with "award winning" faith. Yet when you think about it, you may know a few people who deserve to be singled out for their faith. Who are they? How does their faith show itself? How does their faith help make a difference in your life?** You may want to use whatever time is left to write short notes to the people kids list.

THE HALL OF FAME GAME

People Who Deserve to Be in THE SPORTS HALL OF FAME

A

R

G

W

K

Characters Who Deserve to Be in THE CARTOON HALL OF FAME

F

L

H

Q

U

People Who Deserve to Be in THE COMEDY HALL OF FAME

S

N

B

O

People Who Deserve to Be in THE MUSIC HALL OF FAME

Y

M

C

V

I

People Who Deserve to Be in THE BIBLE HALL OF FAME

J

E

D

P

Z

HEBREWS 12

Weight to Go

We must get rid of anything that weighs us down as we "run the race" of the Christian life, and accept God's discipline to make us stronger. We have been welcomed into God's presence and must not refuse Him.

(Needed: Props for a relay race)

Divide into teams and have a relay race. But "rig" the race by giving one team a handicap so severe that it prevents that team from winning. For instance, one team might use a pencil as a baton while the other is forced to "hand off" a bowling ball, a handful of eggs, or a heavy weight from a home gym. Or you could do the hold-a-spoon-in-your-mouth-with-an-egg-in-the-spoon relay, but require one team to hold two spoons (and eggs). Later, as the disadvantaged team complains of the unfairness of the race, ask how we sometimes "run the race" as Christians with self-imposed handicaps. That's one of the main topics in Hebrews 12.

DATE I USED THIS SESSION _____ GROUP I USED IT WITH _____

NOTES FOR NEXT TIME_____

_____

_____

1. If you were playing in a statewide baseketball tournament, how would you feel if no one from your school or family came to watch? How could having a cheering section influence your performance?

2. In our spiritual "race," it's important to have a lot of support—and we do. The faithful people of God who have gone before are cheering us on (vs. 1). Who are some other people who support your efforts at being a better Christian?

3. Why does it help to keep our eyes focused on Jesus (vss. 2, 3)? (If we don't, we tend to think we're running for no purpose. By focusing on Jesus and remembering what He's already been through, we aren't so likely to quit.)

4. When it comes to the spiritual race, which of the following is closest to your attitude?

• "Why knock myself out? I'll get to heaven no matter how fast I run."

• "Racing is for pastors and missionaries, not average people like me."

• "I'm running the *real* race for grades and a job, not some invisible one."

• "I tried running the race, but I got tired and quit."

• "I'm running, but I don't seem to be getting anywhere."

• "I think I'm making some progress in the race."

• "I don't get the whole 'racing' idea."

5. Like the Hebrew Christians, we don't usually have to bleed for what we believe (vss. 4). Do you think you ever will? Why or why not? Has your "struggle against sin" ever caused you any pain? (This might include embarrassment, having to give up some habits or friendships, the frustration of resisting temptation, etc.)

6. Verses 5-13 talk about discipline, comparing God to our human fathers. **What word best sums up the discipline you've gotten from your parents? How might you be different if your parents had never disciplined you? How is God's discipline different from that of your parents?** (God never makes mistakes; His discipline is always for our good.)

7. How can hardship and discipline be encouraging? (The hardships we face as Christians are proof that God treats us as His children. Parents allow you to ride bikes, drive cars, play ball, and do any number of fun activities with risks that could cause pain. They know that occasional painful lessons are part of the growing-up process. In the same way, God allows us to face certain hardships as disciplines that make us stronger.)

8. On a scale of 1 to 10 (10 highest), how does our group live up to each of the standards in verse 14-17—being at peace with each other, being holy, having no "bitter roots," practicing sexual purity toward each other, and being godly?

9. Which of the two "mountains" described (vss. 18-21 and vss. 22-24) **expresses how most people think of God? Which describes your relationship with Him?** (Press for specific examples of how kids have experienced fear, a sense of distance, joy, etc., as they've tried to relate to God.)

10. How do verses 25-29 fit with what we just read about not needing to be afraid? (We *do* need to be afraid if we reject God's Word. Jesus, our mediator, lets us experience joy and peace in relationship to God the Father, but we still need "reverence and awe" for the Almighty.)

We all find ourselves burdened down by things that keep us from running the Christian race effectively. The reproducible sheet, "Racing Form," illustrates this. After group members "handicap" the race and fill in the things that weigh them down, discuss: **Why do you carry extra burdens around? Are there any you can get rid of this week . . . or today? How can you get rid of them?**

Racing Form

And they're off! Who do you think will win this marathon? Here are the runners:

Name: Bart Simpleton
Strengths: Strong legs, good balance.
Weakness: For some reason he carries a 75-pound giant-screen TV on his head all the time; apparently unable to put it aside in order to run the race.

Name: Andrea Macaroni
Strengths: Great stamina, fine muscle tone.
Weakness: Carries a huge grudge against the other runners; refuses to get near them, so tends to stay at least 50 yards behind.

Name: Desiree Galoot
Strengths: Sharp eyes, winning attitude.
Weakness: Tends to be distracted by any good-looking guy who runs by; carries around a lot of fantasies that cause her to wander off the track.

Name: M.C. Hacksaw
Strengths: Good form and follow-through.
Weakness: Carries 150 pounds of textbooks at all times; thinks the finish line is at Genius University, so tends to run in the wrong direction.

Name: Flicka IV
Strengths: Sure-footed on a muddy track; eats inexpensive food.
Weakness: Eats so much inexpensive food that she's gained 750 pounds; won't drink Ultra Slim-Fast because it doesn't come in alfalfa flavor.

Name: Slats Domino
Strengths: Has been training every day for two years; accepts the discipline of his coach; says he's in the race for the long haul.
Weakness: Used to have back trouble, but felt much better when he stopped carrying around an expensive car on his shoulders.

Now fill in some information about yourself. What strengths do you bring to running the spiritual race? What weaknesses are you weighing yourself down with?

Your Strengths: _____

Your Weaknesses: _____

"Let us throw off everything that hinders and the sin that so easily entangles, and let us run with perseverance the race marked out for us" (Hebrews 12:1).

An Offering You Can't Refuse

The writer of Hebrews encourages us to live out our faith in our relationships to others and by continually offering our praise to God.

(Needed: Two envelopes; team prize [optional])

Before the session, copy and cut apart two sets of the words on the reproducible sheet, "It All Fits Together." Cut so that each word is on a separate slip of paper. Put each set of words in a separate envelope. When the meeting starts, give a complete, cut-up set of words to each of two teams. Have teams compete to see which can first assemble these 13 commands from Hebrews 13. Make sure each team has a New International Version of the Bible for help. (Answers: Keep on loving each other; entertain strangers; remember those in prison; keep the marriage bed pure; stay free from the love of money; be content with what you have; remember your leaders; don't be carried away by strange teachings; bear the disgrace Jesus bore; continually offer to God a sacrifice of praise; don't forget to do good; share with others; obey your leaders.) Award a prize to the winning team if you like. Discuss the challenge of keeping so many commands straight.

DATE I USED THIS SESSION _____ GROUP I USED IT WITH _____

NOTES FOR NEXT TIME _____

_____

_____

1. Have you ever wanted to tell someone more than you had time or space to say? What happened? How did you feel?

2. The writer of Hebrews had a lot of important instructions to give his readers, and packed them into chapter 13. When you get a lot of instructions at the same time—maybe when you're learning a game or starting a new job—how do you remember them? (Write them down, watch somebody else follow them and imitate that person, etc.) **What might help you remember the instructions in this chapter?**

3. What could the writer possibly mean by "entertaining angels" (vs. 2)? (Reflect on what Jesus said about help given to "the least of these" credited as help given to Him [Matthew 25:31-40].)

4. How are some of your peers "in prison" (vs. 3)? (Some may literally be in jail; others are trapped in bad home situations, in alcohol or drug addiction, etc. Note that the instruction says to empathize with such people—not to subject ourselves to the same problems.)

5. You may be a little young for marriage (vs. 4), but what are some ways to be "pure" on a date? What places and situations should you avoid on a date?

6. How would a teenager who has a lot of money show that he or she loves it (vss. 5, 6)? How would a teenager who has very little money show that he or she loves money? How can we get free of the love of money? (If we're really content with God's presence in our lives, the lure of money won't be nearly as strong.)

7. Can you think of someone who has had a strong influence on your spiritual growth (vs. 7)? (Allow time to respond.) **Why do you suppose the writer wrote about Jesus Christ (vs. 8) right after talking about leaders?** (Our role models die and are replaced. But Jesus doesn't change, nor does truth. We should be thankful for the spiritual truths we've been taught, as well as for our teachers, because these things will stand the test of time.)

8. The challenge for the Hebrew Christians was not to drift back to their old ways of worship and sacrifice (vss. 9-14). **How can we offer the new kind of sacrifice God wants (vss. 15, 16)?** (The "sacrifice of praise" means offering ourselves for His glory and service. When we choose to honor God, we'll have to "sacrifice" some of our own desires.)

9. How do we need to obey our spiritual leaders today (vss. 17-19)? **If our pastor told you that you needed to do one of the following, what would be your reaction:** (a) study the Bible more; (b) break up with someone who wasn't a Christian; (c) see a counselor about a problem that had been bothering you?

10. If you were making a list of "everything good for doing [God's] will" (vs. 21) **that you thought you would need, what three things would be at the top of your list?**

Help your group members narrow in on what it means to offer a "sacrifice of praise" (vs. 15) with the following discussion.

• **"Sacrifice" means giving something up. If you're going to praise God more often, you'll have to do something else less. What would you be willing to sacrifice to provide ten more minutes a day for praising God?**

• **To praise God, you need to know what to praise Him for. What are some praiseworthy things you know about God?**

• **God doesn't just want lip service (vs. 16). What object, time, or information could you share with someone else this week as a sacrifice of praise?**

If possible, conclude the discussion with group praise—sentence prayer, songs, making banners, etc.

IT ALL FITS TOGETHER

KEEP *on* **LOVING EACH** other **ENTERTAIN**

strangers *remember* **THOSE** in <u>**PRISON**</u> **KEEP**

the *Marriage* **bed** PURE **stay** *free*

from the **love** *of* **money** be

CONTENT *with* <u>*what*</u> **YOU** *have* **REMEMBER**

your LEADERS **don't** be CARRIED **away**

By strange TEACHINGS **bear** *the* Disgrace

Jesus bore *continually* OFFER TO **God**

a SACRIFICE *of* **PRAISE** don't f o r g e t

to do GOOD *share* with **others**

OBEY *your* LEADERS